Change us not God

Biblical meditations on the death of Jesus

ISBN: 978-0-9824092-9-9

WCF Publishing
wcfoundation.org

Table of Contents

1. Introduction 1

The goal of this study is to try to recapture the simplicity of salvation as taught by Jesus and his apostles. We explore an exciting idea: that the death of Jesus is supposed to have a very real impact on each one of us — it is intended to change us! Any attempt at understanding the work of Jesus requires thoughtfulness and humility from each of us. It is a huge topic, and can provoke tension between us if we are not careful. It is holy ground.

2. Atonement theories 6

There have been many theories of salvation, including ransom, satisfaction, and substitution. Substitution is a legal theory that was formulated in the thirteenth century and is widespread today.

3. Dissecting substitution 11

The substitution theory fails for many reasons: it is unjust, it puts the problem in the wrong place, the penalty is wrong, there would be nothing left to forgive, and it would imply universal salvation. In particular, substitution is a transactional theory rather than a moral theory. Yet atonement is about addressing a problem with us, not a problem that God has.

4. To change us 17

The actual physical death of Jesus was not a metaphysical transaction designed to change things in heaven. Rather, it was to change things within ourselves, to make us be different. It is the beginning of a process or event in which we must participate. It inspires us to share in the sacrifice Jesus made.

5. Bore our sins 23

The crucifixion was an act of murder — an act of sin — even though God asked Jesus to endure it. He faced and bore the full force of our sins, and left us in no doubt about the destructiveness of sin. We can no longer make excuses for our behavior.

6. Resurrection..32

If Jesus had stayed dead, then we would still be in our sins. He was raised from the dead by his Father so that we too might walk in newness of life. We are rescued through his resurrection, because we need a living Lord.

7. Gave his life 38

When the Scriptures say that Jesus gave his life, it means he gave all of it, not just that he died. Because he loved the Father and the people given into his care, Jesus devoted his life to bringing us into life.

8. Blood sacrifice..44

Blood is a symbol of life, so blood sacrifices were symbolically about the giving of life. God wants us to be like Jesus and each to be willing to give up every aspect of our life so that we might truly find it.

9. Mercy, not appeasement..49

The technical English word 'propitiation' (appeasement) is often used to describe the purpose of the death of Jesus. But it is a mistranslation of a family of words in the original of the New Testament. Rather, the idea behind these words is merciful forgiveness, not appeasement.

10. Covering 56

When God provides a covering, he does it for our sake, as a way to give us confidence; from the first literal covering of Adam and Eve, through to the symbolic covering of Christ. He does so to help us overcome our fear and shame, so that we may have courage in coming to his throne of grace.

11. Law and Christ 63

The Law of Moses is a shadow of the realities found in Christ. He is the original, the Law is the derivation. In particular, taking his own life-blood as the offering, Jesus entered the real tabernacle in heaven, an event which the Old Testament imagery was designed to represent.

12. Salvation before Christ..69

The principles for salvation across the Old and New Testaments are the same. Faith was the basis for salvation in the Old Testament, just as it is in the New. While the details of worship may be different, God has always sought to win our hearts and minds.

13. The purpose of God..74

The paradox of the Glory of God: to balance the choice of when to forgive and when to condemn. God wants to build a society of beings who love one another through their free will, and he uses that choice as the basis of his judgment.

14. Righteousness and sin 82

The essence of sin is destructiveness, while the essence of righteousness is to love others truly. God wants us to admit that we are sinners, so that he may work in our lives to have us overcome our natural inclinations.

15. The salvation process 89

Salvation starts with God declaring both our sin and his love. When we agree and want to be different, he freely forgives us and liberates us from our guilt. We trust in him and participate in his work of transforming us, which he completes in resurrection and judgment.

16. Savior...98

God is our savior, but because of fear people like us have always needed God to work through intermediaries, to appoint representatives to speak for him. So God has provided the ultimate prophet, Jesus; he is one of us, yet he speaks perfectly for God. He is our savior.

17. Prophet leaders..104

Prophet leaders were appointed to rescue the people from their destructive ways and urge them to listen to what God was saying. Mighty though they were, these prophets were always less than perfect. God still had to intervene with his own voice, his own right arm, Jesus his son.

18. Humanity of Jesus 110

Jesus was truly a human being, including having to wrestle with real and forceful temptation. The wilderness temptations came as a preparation for the rigors of the temptations that would arise in life circumstances, as evidenced by the events at Nazareth.

19. Temptations in life 116

Jesus experienced challenging temptations in the feeding of the 5000, and ultimately at Gethsemane. He faces the temptation head on during that final evening, and his victory over the flesh is won that night.

20. In the image of God..123

Jesus is the human manifestation of everything God is and says. But it didn't come to him for free: he underwent his own personal discipline, and was perfected in the process. He is in the image of God. He is the word of God.

21. Savior Judge 132

Through the disciplines of his life, Jesus came to manifest God perfectly. Consequently, he has been appointed as savior and judge on God's behalf. He is entrusted with every aspect of the salvation process, fulfilling God's will in rescuing us from death.

22. The present work of Jesus...139

The popular idea that Jesus is interceding with God on our behalf runs into many problems when it is examined in detail. Jesus himself denies that this is his role, and it is inconsistent with who he is, and with the authorities that have already been granted to him.

23. Jesus as mediator 145

The Bible never describes Jesus as our mediator, bringing our demands to God. Rather, it consistently describes him as the mediator of a new covenant, bringing the message from God to humanity. The direction is always: from God, to humanity.

24. Practical intercession 151

Intercession happens when Jesus gets directly and personally involved in our lives, and helps us to overcome despite our weakness. This is seen in a practical example of Jesus interceding in the case of Peter.

25. Jesus as priest 158

As priest, Jesus' main role is to be in our lives, to instruct us, to represent God's way to us, and to rescue us from the destructiveness of sin.

26. Book of life 164

John has a vision of the tabernacle in heaven in which Jesus, the Lamb, presents his blood as a mark of his submission and commitment. In acknowledgment of his accomplishment, and the awful price he paid, he is given the right to open the Book of Life. This Book records the names of those who are being saved. It is being written now.

27. Confidence in the judgment 172

Our relationship with Christ gives us confidence that our names are written in the Book of Life, despite our weaknesses and imperfections. The completeness of his love for us gives us overwhelming confidence about his judgment towards us.

28. Afterword 178

29. Index of Quotations 183

30. Subject Index 186

Introduction

I've often wondered why Jesus died.

It is the pivotal event in history, inspiring and awesome. But it's also hard to understand.

Of course, at one level it is easy. By definition, a Christian believes that Jesus died for our sins, that he rose again, and that he saves us. Here's how Paul puts it:

> *For what I received I passed on to you as of first importance: that Christ died for our sins according to the Scriptures, that he was buried, that he was raised on the third day according to the Scriptures. (1 Cor 15:3-4)*

And a corresponding statement from Peter:

> *For Christ died for sins once for all, the righteous for the unrighteous, to bring you to God. (1 Pet 3:18)*

This is what we might call the *doctrine of salvation.* It affirms that Jesus is savior — more, that he is *my savior* — and that his death was key to saving us.

Essentially, that is all we need: a childlike acceptance of the provision of God.

But we can gain great spiritual benefit in understanding the death of Christ at a much deeper level, in going beyond the basic statement of the doctrine, and in coming to understand *how* his death brings us to God.

So why did he die? Why did Jesus experience such a horrible death? And why didn't God pick some other way for us to be saved?

Theories

Throughout the last 2,000 years, Christians have struggled with this question. Very many theories have been developed to try to explain why Jesus died, and to say just how his death is tied into our salvation. Yet, despite all this effort, in my experience it's really quite hard to find explanations that stand up to close examination.

When I was learning the gospel, and for quite a long time afterwards, I kept asking people, 'Why did Jesus have to die?' I was looking for some basic principles that would be sufficient for building an understanding of salvation. Ideally, they would have been "self-evident truths" — things which make sense in and of themselves — and these truths would connect together to provide a robust explanation.

I got plenty of explanations. Many were quite helpful at providing insight and encouragement. But I found none that seemed to have a really solid foundation. Instead, all the explanations I received were in terms of metaphors and allegories, or were attempts to reason by analogy, but with little evidence to demonstrate why the particular analogies were valid.

Of course, it's possible that God doesn't *expect* us to understand.

Perhaps the crucifixion at Golgotha is too grand for us to be able to grasp, and we are expected simply to look on in wonder. Or perhaps God has deliberately chosen to make the reasons for the death of Jesus complicated and confusing. In either case, if an honest study of the Bible led us to either conclusion, we would have to accept it.

But in fact the Bible does try very hard to explain to us why Jesus died.

The goal of this study is to try to recapture the simplicity of salvation as taught throughout the Bible. We will study the atonement (as it is often called), away from the metaphors, allegories and symbolisms. We will lay aside all analogies, and will instead concentrate simply on finding the basic principles.

In doing so, we will come across an exciting idea: that the death of Jesus was not so much about a transaction taking place in heaven with God, but that it is an event that is intended to have a very real impact on each one of us — even today. It is intended to change us, not God!

How to read this book

There are a couple of ways that you can read this study. You could just pick it up by yourself and zip through it. But I think you may get more from it if you read it more slowly and pause to think about the discussion topics at the end of each section.

In fact, that's probably the best way, especially if you can get together with others who are also interested in the topic, and read it together. Each of the sections is designed to be read aloud in about twenty minutes or so. If you put aside an hour together, you may cover one to two sections, depending on how much you end up discussing the ideas they provoke.

Almost all the Bible passages are quoted verbatim to make for an easy reading process. However, if you wonder about how or why I am interpreting a passage a particular way, please get your Bible out. Then you can read a larger section to see whether the context is consistent with what I have suggested.

I have used the New International Version (NIV) as the main Bible translation, because of its clarity and vibrancy. There are places where that is insufficient, in which case we will explore other translations, or even dig into the underlying Hebrew or Greek text.

This is a good place to comment on my assumptions about how to study the Bible, as different people have different beliefs about this.

I view the Bible as a collection of writings that spiritually-minded people wrote as they were prompted by an active and communicating God. Through his guidance, these writings are entirely trustworthy — at least in their original form — and have a coherence and timeless relevance, while also bearing the mark of the individuality of their writers, and of the specific historic and social circumstances in which they were written.

This assumption has a number of interesting consequences.

First, we should not read the Bible as if it were written to us directly. It wasn't. It was written within many different specific historical contexts, addressing many different specific circumstances. To be true to the Bible, we have to do our best to understand what each of the writers was trying to convey to his particular audience, and then apply the corresponding message to ourselves. This necessarily implies that we will have to bring interpretation. We just have to be careful to leave our personal biases at the door when we do so.

Second, because the many writings that make up the Bible have a single guiding author behind them, it makes sense to compare scripture passage with scripture passage, even when they were written hundreds of years apart. If we do so with due care and attention, we can pick up echoes and patterns that occur right across the Bible, and so can come to understand the sweep of teaching that God has revealed to us. In contrast, building doctrines on just a couple of verses can be a dangerous practice!

As may already be clear, I presume most readers to be active Christians. If you are not, I hope you may still enjoy the study, perhaps also seeing some dimensions that are relevant in your life too.

Holy ground

One final note of preamble. Exploring the reasons for Jesus' death can cause all sorts of problems. Communities have divided on this issue, and tragically, history tells us that people have even murdered each other because they had differing views. Yet we are supposed to be trying to grasp the wonder of the death of God's son!

This is holy ground; this is *really holy ground* that we're walking on.

We have to come to this subject with great sensitivity, with honest and deep love for one another, and with a great sense of our inadequacy before our Father and his Son. They have done so much for us, have given so much of themselves. For us to dissect this topic in order to argue and divide over it would go against everything that God has been doing for us.

So, as we take this journey together, please consider the thoughts in this book simply as meditations on the topic. In no way do I intend them to be taken as absolute. Neither should you expect this to be an academic treatise in comparative or systematic theology. Rather, these thoughts are offered with a goal of stimulating spiritual thought, and enriching our understanding of the tremendous work that has been done.

That said, there are times when I write passionately and emphatically. That comes from being caught up in the intensity of the subject. I am keen for you also to feel passionately about these things. And may God help us always to direct that passion in love for each other, never in biting or devouring.

Like Moses, let us take off our shoes, and bow down before the majesty of our Father and the glory of his Son as we are enveloped in their love for us.

Summary

The goal of this study is to try to recapture the simplicity of salvation as taught by Jesus and his apostles. We explore an exciting idea: that the death of Jesus is supposed to have a very real impact on each one of us – it is intended to change us! Any attempt at understanding the work of Jesus requires thoughtfulness and humility from each of us. It is a huge topic, and can provoke tension between us if we are not careful. It is holy ground.

Discussion

1. What do *you* hope to accomplish by exploring the death of Jesus?
2. What concerns or worries might you have about reexamining this subject, and possibly coming to some different conclusions than you had before?
3. Discuss what the difference is between a parable and a literal fact. Try to give some examples from everyday life.
4. What spiritual preparation could you or the group do before embarking on this exploration? Prayer? Fasting? Suggest some ideas to each other.

Atonement theories

We are going to have to begin with some unraveling. Some of the theories about the death of Christ are so widespread that they may be unconsciously taken as fact unless we take the time to notice them, and then reexamine them in the light of Biblical teaching. So that's what we'll start doing now.

First a comment. This section is called Atonement Theories. That sounds grand and maybe complicated. So before we dive in, let's take the mystery out of the words *atone* and *atonement*, because they have come to mean different things to different people. They are words that come with their own baggage.

The origin of *atone* is very simple. According to my dictionary, it was invented by William Tyndale in sixteenth century English, coming from a contraction of the phrase *at one.* Tyndale was trying to express the ideas of forgiveness and reconciliation. So, *atonement* just means *to be united*, or perhaps, *to be reunited.* Since the purpose behind the life and death of Jesus is to reunite human beings with God, the word is very appropriate.

Notice that the word *atone* doesn't imply any mechanism or method. So if you think *sacrifice* whenever you hear the word *atonement*, you may be reading too much into the word. Whenever we use it here, we shall just take it to mean *reuniting*, without any assumption about how that may be accomplished.

Ransom Theory

Historically, one of the earliest technical theories of atonement came from Origen in the third century. He viewed Jesus' death as a ransom for us. In one sense he was right. After all, Jesus himself says:

> *The Son of Man did not come to be served, but to serve, and to give his life as a ransom for many. (Matt 20:28)*

However, Origen interpreted this very literally. He argued that the devil had gained ownership over us, and that God had to find a ransom to pay to the devil to buy our release. That payment, according to his theory, was Jesus.

Though this theory held sway for nearly a thousand years, it falls down on a number of grounds. To start with, it assumes that an evil being could hold God over a barrel, and could be in a position to demand payment for us. This contradicts the absolute supremacy of God.

It gets even worse. In the ransom theory, after paying up, God turns around and perpetrates a swindle! Once the devil released his claim on us, God then raised Jesus from the dead to get him back too!

We won't examine the ransom theory in any more detail than this. Suffice it to say that whatever Jesus had in mind, he probably meant his words metaphorically, rather than as a literal description of a transaction that bought our salvation. After all, the Psalms say:

> *No man can redeem the life of another or give to God a ransom for him. (Ps 49:7)*

Satisfaction Theory

At the start of the twelfth century Archbishop Anselm of Canterbury completely recast the theory of atonement to address the problems he saw with the Ransom Theory. He introduced the Satisfaction Theory*, which is built on the feudal sense of honor and dignity that was very strong in his age: think knights and ladies, and dueling to avenge honor.

Anselm saw our sin as being an affront to God. God has been defrauded the honor due to him, Anselm claimed, so he could not accept us until his righteousness had been satisfied. Satisfaction is about mending what has been broken, paying back what was taken.

There is a moral imbalance in the universe, Anselm said, and it needs to be paid back on behalf of humanity. When Jesus died, he did not pay a debt to Satan but to God.

Anselm's idea was enough to call the Ransom Theory into question, but it didn't provide enough of an explanation to fully satisfy his contemporaries. Thomas Aquinas, for example, considered the

---

* *Cur Deus Homo, 1100 CE.*

Satisfaction Theory insufficient because it emphasized God's honor rather than his holiness and justice. To address this perceived shortcoming, in his unfinished theological treatise* Aquinas introduced the Substitution Theory instead.

Penal Substitution, as the Substitution Theory is properly called, replaces the *honor* aspect of satisfaction with a *legal* theory. It comprehensively replaced the Satisfaction Theory to become the dominant theory within the Catholic church and with the reformers when Protestantism was born.

Substitution Theory

Substitution builds on the idea of the Law of Sin and Death established by God, namely that sin always leads to death. For example,

> *... but you must not eat from the tree of the knowledge of good and evil, for when you eat of it you will surely die. (Gen 2:17)*

> *For the wages of sin is death, but the gift of God is eternal life in Christ Jesus our Lord. (Rom 6:23)*

Rather than viewing this Law as just a natural law (like the Law of Gravity, for example), substitution is the theory that God had established the law as a Legal Requirement, that sin *legally requires* death.

Under this legal requirement, once we sin we are automatically destined for death as a legal imperative, one that not even God can simply move aside. Christ then died in our place (as a *substitute* for us) so that God's legal requirement could be met, without us having to die for our own sin. He bore the punishment that was due to us, the substitutionist would say, so that we are freed from the law that says sin is punished by death.

Whereas the satisfaction theory said that Christ obeyed where we should have obeyed, and this allowed us to become acceptable to God, the substitution theory says that Christ was punished where we should have been punished.

---

* *Summa Theologica, 1265-1274 CE.*

As substitution is the theory of atonement that is most prevalent today, particularly within the evangelical movement, it is worth looking at quite carefully.

The parable of the circus

I once came across a great story that elaborates the substitution idea. The story provides a powerful allegory, and shows both the strengths and weaknesses of the theory of substitution.

> *A father had two sons. One day he heard the circus was coming to town. He said to the boys, "The circus is coming next weekend. If you behave yourselves, we'll all go to the circus and have a good time."*
>
> *The older son behaved himself impeccably throughout the week, a wonderful example of good behavior. Unfortunately, the same could not be said of the younger boy. At the end of the week, the father assessed the situation and said to the younger son, "I would dearly love to take you to the circus, but your behavior hasn't merited it. Even though it upsets me, I'm going to have to live by my word and not take you to the circus."*
>
> *The younger son is absolutely devastated, and there is an impasse. However much they all want the boy to go, the father can't simply say: "You know what? I'm going to forget what I said, you can come to the circus after all!" It would completely negate what the father had said. What can be done?*
>
> *Then the older son comes to the rescue. He says: "Father, I will bear the punishment of the younger son; I will stay home. That way you may take him to the circus. Your word is upheld and we shall achieve what we wanted to accomplish."*
>
> *Suddenly this changes everything! By his generosity and sacrifice, the older son has provided a way forward for the father, and he is able to take the younger boy to the circus without nullifying his word.*

As a young Christian, I found this a very moving story. It captivated me because of the individual sacrifice of the older son. It is very compelling. It even has clear parallels in Scripture, with Judah offering himself in Benjamin's place (Gen 44:33), for example.

For much of the mainstream evangelical movement, I think this story well reflects the process of salvation. We have done everything that merits death. God has said in his righteousness that sin leads to death. We have sinned — it leads to our death. And we would die because God can't simply reverse his word and say, "Let's forget all about that sin stuff. Come into glory after all."

According to substitution, God is at an impasse until he devises a plan so that we won't have to die. In that plan, Jesus says to the Father: "I will take the punishment, the death that is due. I will bear it. Your justice will be vindicated, and you will still be able to accept people into glory."

The main attraction of substitution is that it is very simple and easy to understand. As a young Christian, I found it was an explanation of the process of salvation that made some sense to me. But over time I began to see both its limitations and unpleasant implications. It has some very serious shortcomings!

We'll look at some of these in the next section and beyond.

Summary

There have been many theories of salvation, including ransom, satisfaction, and substitution. Substitution is a legal theory that was formulated in the thirteenth century and is widespread today.

Discussion

1. Before you had read this section, what did you think the word *atonement* meant (if anything)?
2. What ideas have you heard from other people about the reasons for Jesus' death? Why do *you* think Jesus died?
3. What is the difference between natural law, and legal law?
4. What do you see as the strengths and weaknesses of the substitution theory? Start with an analysis of the circus parable, and then consider the substitution theory itself.
5. What aspects do all these atonement theories have in common?

Dissecting substitution

If the substitution theory is understood to be just a metaphor, then perhaps it can help us appreciate some aspects of salvation. But instead, the substitution theory is accepted by many Christians as if it were *literal truth.*

Remember that it's important to see metaphor as metaphor, symbol as symbol and parable as just parable, not the reality itself. So let's see now why substitution cannot be taken literally.

We'll do this by treating the theory of substitution as if it were literal truth, and then showing what contradictions arise as a result. Here are five serious challenges.

1. Substitution is unjust

The first problem of substitution is one of justice. Or, rather, injustice.

Since when is it a mark of justice to punish the wrong person? The whole notion of substitution is based on the idea that the justice of God has to be upheld, and so he does what? He *punishes the wrong man!*

Do you see how it erodes the very core of the idea of justice? The Bible never considers it just or right to punish the wrong person. A major theme of Isaiah's whole prophecy is to condemn those who take bribes, who allow the guilty to go unpunished, or who punish the innocent. For example,

> *Woe to those ... who acquit the guilty for a bribe, but deny justice to the innocent. (Is 5:22-23)*

Proverbs has quite a bit to say on the topic too:

> *Acquitting the guilty and condemning the innocent — the LORD detests them both. (Prov 17:15)*

Does it make sense that God might then go and do so himself? Of course not. God states the principle directly through Ezekiel:

> *The soul who sins is the one who will die. The son will not share the guilt of the father, nor will the father share the guilt of the son. The righteousness of the righteous man will be credited to him, and the wickedness of the wicked will be charged against him. (Ezek 18:20)*

Substitution is a theory of legal justice, but contains a legal injustice at its core.

2. The penalty is wrong

Second, note that the penalty Jesus bore is not the one we were condemned with. The penalty of sin is death itself, *not* simply the process of dying. The penalty of sin is eternal separation from God, it is eternal destruction, oblivion — for ever. That punishment has not been borne by Jesus.

Because Jesus is no longer dead, he has not borne the true penalty of sin. He *tasted* death, certainly. He experienced the agonies of death, went into the grave and was dead for three days. But if he was supposed to be bearing *our punishment*, God should have left him dead.

Did God then change his mind and decide not to punish him with the punishment that was due to us after all? In the circus parable, it's as if the father says to the son, "You stay at home and I'll take the younger brother," and then, halfway to the circus he telephones home and says, "I've changed my mind. Come after all!" He's not bearing the punishment.

Substitution is a legal theory, but it contains a mismatched penalty at its core.

3. Nothing left to forgive

Third, substitution leaves no room for forgiveness.

Suppose Bob owes me money. I keep saying, "Come on, Bob, you owe me five bucks. Pay up! Pay up!" Then Alice hears this and says to me, "Hey, I'll give you the five bucks that Bob owes you." Would it be fair for me now to go to Bob and say: "I *forgive* you your debt!" Not at all!

Alice has already *paid* the debt; there's nothing left to be forgiven. It's all been dealt with.

Do you see the implications for salvation? If Jesus has paid the debt, if he has satisfied the legal requirement, where is the need for forgiveness? There's no role for it at all; the debt has been paid! Yet again and again and again, the Scriptures say that we come to God through forgiveness. For example:

> *If we confess our sins, he is faithful and just and will forgive us our sins and purify us from all unrighteousness. (1 John 1:9)*

We have to conclude therefore that there is a real debt outstanding! God says: "I forgive!" But substitution would say it's been paid, and hence there's nothing left to forgive.

4. Salvation would be universal

Fourth, if Christ has fully borne the punishment due to sinners, if he has paid the price and earned salvation on behalf of sinners, then there's no reason why anybody should be condemned at God's judgment. Or put the other way around, why would God condemn any of us if Christ has removed the whole legal basis for any of us being condemned? There would be no reason. If the theory of substitution was true, then it would lead logically to a conclusion that salvation should be universal.

But this is a problem. Most Christians agree that the Bible is quite clear that there is going to be a separation between those who are saved, and those who are not. To take just one example, Daniel says:

> *Multitudes who sleep in the dust of the earth will awake: some to everlasting life, others to shame and everlasting contempt. (Dan 12:2)*

Salvation is not universal, so the substitution theory cannot be an accurate description of the mechanism of salvation.

5. Substitution puts the problem in the wrong place

The final problem, and this is a big one, is one of shifting the blame.

We have a great tendency to blame others, to focus on someone else as the one having a problem. It's a natural human act to say: "You know what? It's not really *our* problem! It's really God's problem."

The theory of substitution falls into this trap. It says that the real problem with salvation is that God was in a legal fix, that Jesus had to die to get God out of the legal problems. It allows us to say, "The problem is not with me, it's with God!"

In fact, all the theories of atonement we described in the previous section fail in this same way:

- God found himself needing to ransom us from the devil,
- God's honor was upset, or
- God found himself in a legal bind.

The real problem, of course, is not with God, the problem has *never* been with God. The real problem is with us! The real problem is our opposition to God — opposition and rebellion in my heart, in your heart! *That's* where the challenge is, the rebelliousness of the human being. So that's where the work of salvation has to be focused.

> *Shall we go on sinning so that grace may increase? By no means! We died to sin; how can we live in it any longer? Or don't you know that all of us who were baptized into Christ Jesus were baptized into his death? (Rom 6:1-3)*

In other words, the real purpose of the death of Christ was not to change God, but to change *us!"*

Understanding this shifts our whole perspective by introducing a radically different possibility from what we may have had before. In my own spiritual development, I had wrestled with all the *transactional* theories, but it had never occurred to me to question the very idea whether the death of Christ was a transaction at all!

As I read Scripture more and more, I came to see that the death of Christ was not designed to deal with *God's* difficulties; it was designed to make *me* different! It is to change me!

This is not being self-centered. It's saying: "The *problem* is here with me. Whatever the death of Christ is designed to accomplish, it is designed to accomplish it by *changing me*, where the problem actually lies.

This approach to understanding the death of Christ is sometimes described as a moral influence interpretation, because it addresses the moral problem of sin: the damage sin does to us and to other people.

The French Abbott Peter Abelard was an early proponent* of this approach. We won't necessarily follow the details of Abelard's construction, but will rather connect with the Biblical writings themselves.

Refocus

There is a theme which will come up repeatedly as we proceed through these studies, and it is this: that biblical teaching often gets turned around, shifting the focus from our need to change and grow and supposing that God is the one who needs to be different.

Substitution is our first example. It says that God was in a legal bind, that Jesus' death was designed to change things in heaven. But the problem is not in heaven. It's here on earth. It is in my heart, and in your heart.

This is the direction we'll pursue through these studies to see what we can learn, and how we can grow by it. Note, however, that the substitution theory is so pervasive in our culture, that it is likely to influence our thinking, even if we don't take it on board wholesale. Elements of it can creep in and affect our understanding.

Summary

The substitution theory fails for many reasons: it is unjust, it puts the problem in the wrong place, the penalty is wrong, there would be nothing left to forgive, and it would imply universal salvation. In particular, substitution is a transactional theory rather than a moral theory. Yet atonement is about addressing a problem with us, not a problem that God has.

Discussion

1. Discuss which of the five objections to substitution you found more or less convincing?
2. Consider the parable of the lost son in Luke 15:11-25. Imagine modifying it to teach substitution explicitly. Someone have a go at telling the modified version to the group.
3. How important is it for us to pursue sinlessness in our lives? Why?

---

* *Expositio in Epistolam AD Romanos, Peter Abelard (1079 – 1142)*

4. How have the observations in this section caused you to think again about the death of Jesus (if at all)?

To change us

Substitution and other transactional theories of atonement all lay the need for Christ's death at God's feet. According to these theories, God needed a way to satisfy his honor, or to address issues of legality, and the way he chose was to require Jesus to die by a horrendously cruel form of execution.

Moreover, we have seen that the substitution theory is incompatible with other things we believe about God, such as his justice, omnipotence, love, forgiveness, and so on. So there must be some other reason for Jesus' death.

Ultimately, the problem of salvation is not in heaven with God — the real problem is here with us; it is with me and with you. The problem is Sin, and our addiction to it. God doesn't need to change *his* situation. It is *our* hearts and minds that need to be different. So this is where we shall look to understand the reasons for the death of Jesus.

I am going to propose that there are just two reasons for his death;

1. To change us; and
2. To perfect Jesus himself.

We'll explore (1) over the next dozen sections or so, and then come back to (2) starting with the section entitled Savior on page 98.

Love and obey

We'll start with some words of Jesus himself, spoken the evening he was arrested. About one-third of John's gospel record records the events and conversations of this one evening! It's quite astonishing.

If you open your Bible and explore things a bit, you will see that the last supper takes place amongst the events of John 13, and that in chapter 14, Jesus starts an outpouring of teachings that lasts many chapters.

During this teaching, Jesus and his disciples leave the upper room, cross the Kidron Valley, and start climbing Mount Olives heading for the Garden of Gethsemane. All the while Jesus continues to teach. He must have considered these teachings particularly important, given that he selects them for this very critical time. Here's what he says:

> *I will not speak with you much longer for the Prince of this world is coming. He has no hold on me, but the world must learn that I love the Father and that I do exactly what my Father has commanded me (John 14:30-31).*

I love the NIV translation here. It seems to capture the sense of the original text very well. We are now only about twelve hours before the crucifixion, and Jesus explains to his disciples what is going on. *The world is being taught a double lesson*, he says. The world *must learn* that (a) I love the Father and (b) that I do exactly what my Father has commanded me.

If we want a commentary of the purpose of the crucifixion from the lips of Jesus himself, then we should highlight this verse. It may not reflect the whole story, of course, but it is the aspect he chooses to emphasize just a few short hours before his death. He does not speak about a transaction in heaven. Rather, he highlights an impact on earth: *the world must learn something* from what is about to occur.

Continue in faith

Let's look at a passage from Paul's letter to the Colossians:

> *Once you were alienated from God and were enemies in your minds because of your evil behavior. But now he has reconciled you by Christ's physical body through death to present you holy in his sight, without blemish and free from accusation... (Col 1:21-22)*

If we stopped reading here, we might be excused for drifting into a substitutionary transactional view; just from this verse it sounds as if something might have been sorted out for God by the death of Christ. But let's continue:

> *... if you continue in your faith, established and firm, not moved from the hope held out in the gospel. (Col 1:23)*

You see the point Paul is making? The death of Christ is effective '*if* you continue...' The implication is that whatever the death of Christ accomplishes, it does so only with our participation. Or put the other way around, if the death of Christ does not effect a new and consistent life-direction in us, then it is ineffectual. We have to 'continue' in a life of faithful holiness, in a life of devotion to God.

According to Paul, Christ's death initiates a way of life for us. Contrary to our initial impression, Paul is not presenting it as some mystical event that took place and suddenly we are saved! Rather, it is an event that is bound up with our participation.

Follow the example of Jesus

Here's another example of the same teaching, this time from Peter.

> *To this you were called, because Christ suffered for you, leaving you an example, that you should follow in his steps. (1 Pet 2:21)*

The content of this is remarkably like Jesus' words earlier: the world must *learn* something. Peter heard those words and took them to heart. Jesus, he says, is expecting us to learn from his example. As a result of what he did, Jesus is expecting us to become something different. Notice that there's no hint of substitution here, of Jesus being a sacrifice *instead* of us. Quite the reverse. Jesus is calling us to *join in* his sacrifice.

Here's Paul again on the topic.

> *I want to know Christ and the power of his resurrection and the fellowship of sharing in his sufferings, becoming like him in his death and so, somehow, to attain to the resurrection from the dead. (Phil 3:10)*

Again, no suggestion here of Christ dying instead of us: he describes Jesus' death as something to participate in: I want the fellowship of *sharing* in Christ's sufferings, becoming like him in his death.

Golgotha was not simply something that happened "over there" — such that some mystical rite was performed 2,000 years ago and now we're okay. Rather it is something that requires me to participate. "Take up your cross," Jesus says, "and follow me!" (Matt 16:24) Or, as we've just read here in Peter's first letter, "Christ suffered for you, leaving you an example so that you should follow in his steps."

Without our response and participation, the death of Christ is irrelevant and useless. His death was intended to reach us, to make us responsive, to enable us to hear God calling.

The death of Jesus was necessary because we were so blind that we couldn't see what God had been trying to tell us through the prophets. Christ died to cut through our stubbornness. His death was not about changing God, not changing some kind of legal landscape, or trying to resolve some legal or technical difficulty that God faced. It was to change us, to address *our* limitations, flaws and weaknesses.

Reasons for Jesus' death

In my reading of the Bible I have been driven to the conclusion that *the actual physical death of Christ released no metaphysical principle of salvation.* By *metaphysical principle* I mean no abstract principle of legality, honor, or payment, or anything else, was a barrier to God being able to forgive us. We will see that God could always forgive us.

So what was the purpose behind Jesus' death?

As stated at the start of the chapter, I propose that the Bible gives us two fundamental reasons for Jesus' death.

1. His death is supposed to have a profound and transforming effect on us. It is the beginning of a process in which we must thoroughly participate, and,
2. His personal sacrifice played a major role in the development and perfecting of Christ himself.

Both of these reasons are practical, living in the world of cause and effect. Neither of them are abstractly metaphorical or transactional.

This proposition claims that the death of Christ was an event designed by God with natural consequences through cause and effect; those consequences affecting any of us who are willing to be affected by it, and profoundly affecting Jesus himself.

This is a bold proposition because most Christians were brought up on the idea that the death of Jesus was exactly about some kind of metaphysical or spiritual transaction, and not about natural cause and effect at all. Consequently, a statement such as *the actual physical death of Christ released no metaphysical principle of salvation* is likely to come across as quite a challenging idea. At the very least, it will cause us to pause while we try to see the implications.

Given our own historical and religious contexts, it is natural to have a sense that there *surely was* something transactional that took place at Jesus' death, that some change took place as far as God was concerned. I certainly thought that way for many years. So I'm very aware that when I propose an understanding like this, I'm on borrowed time! But please bear with me, and see what you think as we work through the study together. Each of us will have to examine for ourselves whether the statement is fair to the weight of Scripture on the topic.

And if that idea is not challenging enough, the idea that Jesus himself benefited in his personal growth and development can seem quite surprising. Maybe even shocking! However, as indicated earlier, it will take us many chapters just to explore the effect that the death of Christ has on us, which means that it will take quite a while before we get to look at the perfecting of Christ. This may be an even more challenging idea to hold in trust, but I don't want us to forget about it, because it turns out to be a critical dimension of Golgotha.

Summary

The actual physical death of Jesus was not a metaphysical transaction designed to change things in heaven. Rather, it was to change things within ourselves, to make us be different. It is the beginning of a process or event in which we must participate. It inspires us to share in the sacrifice Jesus made.

Discussion

1. This section proposes that the death of Jesus is not about changing God but about changing us. What impact does this have on your concept of God and salvation?
2. Discuss whether you found the passages quoted as forming a compelling argument that the death of Jesus is intended to change us.
3. How could our participation in salvation be squared with the idea that we are saved by grace rather than by works?
4. Discuss how you personally can participate in the death of Jesus in your life.
5. Write down the ideas and Bible passages that jump to mind as contradicting this section, i.e. that seem to support the idea that Jesus' death accomplished some kind of transaction in heaven.

Keep these passages on hand as you continue the study, and see if you come to think about them differently.

Bore our sins

In the Bible we find many references to Jesus as a "sacrifice" for our sins. The Law of Moses, which suffuses the Old Testament, was full of sacrifice, so this would have been natural language for the authors of the Bible. It is far less natural for us, so we have to be especially careful what conclusions we draw.

In particular, a superficial reading of the Old Testament might suggest that God *needs* some kind of blood sacrifice to somehow take our sins away; if we have read it this way, then we might naturally presume that Jesus' death is a sacrifice of exactly this kind.

I don't think we should understand Jesus' death in this way.

It will take us a few sections to explore the idea of sacrifice properly, but for now, let's begin with a couple of questions. Pause after each question, and see what your answer is before going on to read more.

Here's the first. Was it God's will that Jesus should submit to death?

This is easy, it's not a trick question. "Yes," is the answer. Whether we understand why or not, it certainly was God's will that Jesus should submit even to the point of death. Isaiah is clear on this.

> *Yet it was the LORD's will to crush him and cause him to suffer. (Is 53:10)*

What's more, Jesus knew it was God's will. He himself quotes the prophecies that predicted Judas' betrayal, and his prayer at Gethsemane was all about submission to God's will.

Let's ask another question. Were the people who killed Jesus doing God's will?

Again, pause and consider this for a moment, because it is a very telling question. What did you answer?

The answer is, "No." They were not doing God's will. The trial, the condemnation, and the crucifixion were all acts of sin. If they were not acts of sin, why would Jesus ask for forgiveness for those involved in the mechanics of the crucifixion (Luke 23:34)?

Moreover, listen to Stephen's condemnation of the role of the religious authorities,

> *You stiff-necked people, with uncircumcised hearts and ears! You are just like your fathers: You always resist the Holy Spirit! Was there ever a prophet your fathers did not persecute? They even killed those who predicted the coming of the Righteous One. And now you have betrayed and murdered him. (Acts 7:51-52)*

Stephen is very explicit. The crucifixion was an act of betrayal and murder; it was a manifestation of their resistance against the holy spirit. It's impossible to read these verses and conclude that the people who killed Jesus were acting righteously and doing God's will.

Peter, similarly, is quite clear that the crucifixion was both within God's will, and equally an act of sin by those who killed him:

> *This man was handed over to you by God's set purpose and foreknowledge; and you, with the help of wicked men, put him to death by nailing him to the cross. (Acts 2:23)*

This isn't as much of a conundrum as it might appear at first sight. An act can be sin for those who participate in it, while still being used by God to accomplish his will.

In fact, we may go further. God often uses sinful acts to accomplish purposes that far transcend those acts, creating purpose out of destruction, beauty out of brutishness. For example, when Joseph was sold to Egypt by his brothers, they were acting out of envy and violent jealousy. Their betrayal was an act of sin, but as an eventual consequence of their action, God rescued them from famine by elevating Joseph to rulership in Egypt. As Joseph said to his brothers,

> *I am your brother Joseph, the one you sold into Egypt! And now, do not be distressed and do not be angry with yourselves for selling me here, because it was to save lives that God sent me ahead of you. (Gen 45:4-5)*

Just because God accomplished a great purpose in the elevation of Joseph does not mean that their treatment of Joseph was any less sinful. It was indeed sin, and yet equally, God wrought a mighty work through their sin.

In fact, this is the core of the Gospel! Out of death and despair, God brings life and hope. That doesn't make death and despair good, but the Good News is that God is most powerfully at work when darkness seems everywhere.

Just think about our own lives. If we ask ourselves what experiences have been most formative, most significant, or life-giving to us, the chances are, that many of us would respond (if we were honest) with stories of distress and pain, rather than of ease and relaxation. They would be stories of adversity, rather than of vacation in the Caribbean. That doesn't make distress and pain good, but it helps us to see that it is precisely in those moments that we are most open to the influence of God.

This is the story of salvation.

Salvation is not through power and influence, through acts of strength and majesty. Whether in our own lives, or in the work of Jesus himself, salvation is through submission and weakness, through humility and poverty.

This is hard to accept. Whereas much Christian teaching is supported by conventional wisdom, through both positive and negative examples, this teaching runs counter to our every instinct. And yet it is our route to true strength. Here's what Paul says:

> *But [Christ] said to me, "My grace is sufficient for you, for my power is made perfect in weakness." Therefore I will boast all the more gladly about my weaknesses, so that Christ's power may rest on me. That is why, for Christ's sake, I delight in weaknesses, in insults, in hardships, in persecutions, in difficulties. For when I am weak, then I am strong. (2 Cor 12:9-10)*

Consider again the two questions we started with and you will see why it is completely reasonable that they have quite different answers. It was God's will that Christ should submit to death, and at the same time, the people who slew him were committing a despicable act of sin. It was murder.

It is extremely helpful to distinguish between these two questions when we think about the death of Christ.

Bore our sins

This is quite a profound observation we've made, that the act of the crucifixion was an act of sin.

This observation should cause us to pause before assuming we can take the Old Testament principle of sacrifice and apply it to Jesus, without taking some care that we're not mixing up roles.

Let's explore an example from Isaiah 53. You probably know the verse very well, whether from Handel's *Messiah*, or elsewhere:

> *We all, like sheep, have gone astray, each of us has turned to his own way; and the LORD has laid on him the iniquity of us all. (Is 53:6)*

At first this verse seems to suggest a ritual in which Jesus had our sins somehow placed upon him, as if God was making him responsible for our sins, even blaming him. The scapegoat in the Law of Moses is a little like this:

> *[Aaron] is to lay both hands on the head of the live goat and confess over it all the wickedness and rebellion of the Israelites — all their sins — and put them on the goat's head. He shall send the goat away into the desert in the care of a man appointed for the task. The goat will carry on itself all their sins to a solitary place; and the man shall release it in the desert. (Lev 16:21-22)*

This whole passage about the scapegoat seems terribly transactional. The Israelites had to provide a goat, and God would let it carry their sin off into the wilderness. No goat, no forgiveness. Yet as we will see in a later section, God was not the slightest bit interested in the goat itself. Rather, this was the only way God could convey to the people of the time the seriousness of sin.

But what of the parallel with Jesus having our sins "laid on" him?

The apparent parallel falls apart when we realize that when Aaron performed the Rite of the Scapegoat, he was fulfilling God's command. Performing this rite was an act of righteousness, not an act of sin. Yet we've already seen that except for Jesus, everyone who was engaged in the killing at Golgotha was engaged in an act of sin. It was murder.

It turns out that the apparent connection between Isaiah 53 and the scapegoat may be an artifact of the translation of Isaiah. The word *laid* comes from the Hebrew root word *pga* (pronounced pa-gah). Some concordance work shows us that the idea of *pga* is actually that of *meeting* or *encountering* rather than any ritual laying on of hands.

So Isaiah 53:6 is likely to be saying something very plain:

> *The Lord had him encounter the iniquity of us all.*

Jesus "faced" the evil in us all, and was killed in the process. He came into our streets, and faced the gang of evil in our neighborhood. God made him confront the evil of us all.

The same Hebrew word occurs later on in Isaiah 53,

> *Therefore I will give him a portion among the great, and he will divide the spoils with the strong, because he poured out his life unto death, and was numbered with the transgressors. For he bore the sin of many, and made intercession for the transgressors. (Is 53:12)*

See if you can guess which English word comes from *pga.* I couldn't. It's quite surprising: it's the word *intercession.* Without a doubt, meeting can be for the sake of pleading with someone, but there's a much plainer translation that seems possible here, namely,

> *He bore the sin of many, he met face-to-face with the transgressors.*

He bore the sins that the people were committing against him. He took the punishment they were meting out. He bore the full force of their sin. It was our sin — sins of people like us — that killed him. Murder.

Who offered Jesus as a sacrifice?

Let's shift to a different question. If Jesus was a sacrifice, who offered him as a sacrifice?

Let's consider some possible answers.

Depending on how we understand the term *sacrifice*, we could say that God offered Jesus as a sacrifice. That is, if sacrifice is understood in the sense of providing, then it was God who provided Jesus.

> *For God so loved the world that he gave his one and only Son, that whoever believes in him shall not perish but have eternal life. For God did not send his Son into the world to condemn the world, but to save the world through him. (John 3:16-17)*

This was foreshadowed in the story about Abraham offering up Isaac:

> *Abraham answered, "God himself will provide the lamb for the burnt offering, my son." And the two of them went on together. (Gen 22:8)*

As God would offer Jesus, so Abraham would offer Isaac. It seems plain that Isaac was a willing sacrifice, and cooperated with Abraham, in that "the two of them went on together." This anticipated what Jesus would do as a willing sacrifice for his Father.

But this is a little abstract. If we understand sacrifice in the sense of the act itself, the actual offering being made, let's consider again: who offered Jesus as a sacrifice?

Did you? Did I? No, of course not.

Did the people who were living in Jesus' time? Again, no. We've already seen that their minds were focused on murder, not reconciliation.

There can really be only one answer to the question. It was *Jesus* who offered Jesus as a sacrifice.

> *Live a life of love, just as Christ loved us and gave himself up for us as a fragrant offering and sacrifice to God. (Eph 5:2)*

That act of submission was the *one act of righteousness* that was taking place in those events at Golgotha. Everyone else involved in the killing that day was engaged in raw sin. Murderous intent.

No excusing sin

Okay, so it was murder. Then what effect can the death of Jesus have on us?

There are many. For a start, it shows us the utter destructiveness of sin.

We see the most righteous, the most beautiful, the most lovely man that ever lived; and law abiding, religious, ethical people — people like you and me — murdered him!

That should be shocking!

It wasn't as if he went into the worst district of the worst town, and faced a gang of thieves who jumped on him and slew him. It was Roman and Jew, civilized and religious people who decided that this man is better dead than alive. Jesus' very life showed them up for what they were, and they couldn't take it. These people, people who were like us, didn't just kill him despite his sinlessness. They killed him *because* he was sinless. He had not the slightest flaw, so they rejected him. It tells us that people like us are actually opposed to true good.

If that doesn't tell us about the sinfulness of sin, we haven't really thought about it.

As disciples, we are holy people. I don't mean in a self-righteous sense; but holy when we let the holiness of our Lord be upon us, allowing his love and peace to reflect itself in practice in our lives. Yet we still have sin within us. We still have temptation; we still have the tendency to sin. You know it, and so do I. The death of Christ forces us to admit that even in people who desire to be holy, sin is still a powerful force. It's incredibly destructive.

We have a tendency to say, "Oh yes, but this sin of mine isn't so bad; I know those sins over there are really bad and I would never do those, but these sins of mine, they're not so bad!"

That's exactly how the governmental and religious communities of Jesus' day felt and behaved. They could easily condemn all sorts of sins and destructive behaviors. Then they took the most wonderful man that has ever lived ...

... and they killed him!

Jesus himself makes this point. When the women are weeping at the sight of him carrying his cross, he turns to them and says:

> *Daughters of Jerusalem, do not weep for me; weep for yourselves and for your children. [...] For if men do these things when the tree is green, what will happen when it is dry? (Luke 23:28,31)*

He is quite clear: even when times are good, people like us can fall into destructive acts; how much worse do we get when things are tough!

We are left with no excuse about the sinfulness of sin. The little sins that I do, the little sins that you do: where will they lead? The sin may be quite mild, we think. No big deal, we think. How wrong we are.

Even those who genuinely desired to be righteous forsook him. All were complicit in his death.

Consider Nicodemus. He was there in the Sanhedrin council the night Jesus was on trial for his life. He was a supporter of Jesus, but secretly, because he was afraid of the politics of the council. By remaining secretive, the most he may have managed to do was to interfere enough with the farce of a trial so that it took all night. He was not willing to stand up and say, "This is wrong!" Because of his cowardice, and the cowardice of the others, that man was slain.

It was no big sin, right?

I think Nicodemus understood how great a sin it was. I think he felt the personal shame profoundly (John 19:38-42).

Summary

The crucifixion was an act of murder — an act of sin — even though God asked Jesus to endure it. He faced and bore the full force of our sins, and left us in no doubt about the destructiveness of sin. We can no longer make excuses for our behavior.

Discussion

1. This section presented arguments that the killing of Jesus was an act of sin. Discuss whether you were convinced by them or not.
2. Why was Jesus murdered? What do the motivations of Jesus' enemies teach you about yourself?
3. In what circumstances do you find yourself excusing your sin?
4. Read the following quotation from Romans. To what extent is Paul's experience reflected in your own life?

What shall we say, then? Is the law sin? Certainly not! Indeed I would not have known what sin was except through the law. For I would not have known what coveting really was if the law had not said, "Do not covet." But sin, seizing the opportunity afforded by the commandment, produced in me every kind of covetous desire. For apart from law, sin is dead. Once I was alive apart from law; but when the commandment came, sin sprang to life and I died. I found that the very commandment that was intended to bring life actually brought death. For sin, seizing the opportunity afforded by the commandment, deceived me, and through the commandment put me to death.

So I find this law at work: When I want to do good, evil is right there with me. For in my inner being I delight in God's law; but I see another law at work in the members of my body, waging war against the law of my mind and making me a prisoner of the law of sin at work within my members. What a wretched man I am! Who will rescue me from this body of death? Thanks be to God — through Jesus Christ our Lord! (Rom 7:7-11, 21-25)

Resurrection

Earlier we proposed that *the actual physical death of Christ released no metaphysical principle of salvation.* That is, there was no magic associated with the act, no transaction that took place in heaven that fulfilled some prerequisite or previous requirement God had for salvation. Instead, we proposed that,

- His death is supposed to have a profound and transforming effect on us, and
- His personal sacrifice played a major role in the development and perfecting of Christ himself.

In this section we'll further explore the core idea that nothing mystical or magical transpired at the moment of Jesus death to secure our salvation. Again, I understand this is likely to be a troubling idea to many of us. I encourage you nonetheless to keep your hearts and minds open to the scriptures we will explore.

Death and life

Look at Romans 4:25, the first part of the verse.

> *He was delivered over to death for our sins.*

First, note that it doesn't say he was sacrificed; just that he was delivered over to death. Second, in light of the last section, I'd like to suggest that we should understand this as: *he was killed by our sins.* It was no act of righteousness to put Jesus to death, any more than it was an act of righteousness to betray him. "The Son of Man must go as the Scriptures have said but woe unto that man," says Jesus (Matt 26:24). It was the same with the death on the cross. Sinners killed Jesus through acting sinfully. Literally.

Of course, when I say that he was killed by our sins, I don't mean it was literally my personal sins, or your personal sins that killed him. But it was literally the sinful acts of people who were just like us. It was our kind of sins that killed him.

So now let's go back, and look at the whole verse:

> *He was delivered over to death for our sins, he was raised to life for our justification. (Rom 4:25)*

What an interesting counterpoint! Delivered to death for our sins, raised to life for our justification. Peter echoes the pattern

> *You killed the author of life, but God raised him from the dead. (Acts 3:15)*

It's the same pattern. We are responsible for the death, but God is responsible for the life.

Yet Paul seems to go further in Romans 4:25. Paul seems to be saying that Jesus was killed because of sinfulness, but that he was raised in order to save us — justification means essentially the same as salvation: it is an assessment by God that we are righteous before him.

Maybe this is just an accidental turn of phrase, just Paul's style of speaking. Perhaps we shouldn't read too much into it? But in fact, it seems as though Paul's choice of words reflect a real intent. These words echo a principle that many other passages make quite clear.

Jesus death is not the whole story

1 Corinthians 15 is one of those passages. I've been reading it all my life, yet there's a verse here that I'd never noticed for the longest time! At least, I had never read carefully enough to take on board what it actually says. It is right in the middle of the section explaining how important the resurrection of Christ is.

> *If Christ is not raised, your faith is futile, you are still in your sins. (1 Cor 15:16)*

Whoa! If Christ has not been raised … we are still in our sins. This verse implies that the death of Jesus *is not sufficient to bring forgiveness*! The death only is not enough.

Pause for a moment and see for yourself that it follows. If the resurrection is necessary to rescue the Corinthians from their sins, then the death alone cannot have been sufficient. See what I mean?

If the substitution theory was literally true, and the death of Christ has paid our debt and freed us, then this verse would make no sense. Under substitution, the death of Christ is sufficient to release us from our sins. But this verse says that the resurrection of Christ is also necessary, otherwise we are still in our sins.

To put it another way, *this verse alone* is sufficient to establish that substitution is an inadequate model of salvation. Instead, this verse tells us that there is something about the *resurrection of Christ* that frees us from our sins.

Isn't it a fascinating verse?! I'd never noticed it before!

Jesus' resurrection is essential

Maybe it's just Paul who states things this way? But no, it's not. Let's look at Peter, another famous chapter, another verse that we possibly read frequently.

> *This water symbolizes baptism that now saves you also, not the removal of dirt from the body, but the pledge of a good conscience towards God. It saves you by the resurrection of Jesus Christ. (1 Pet 3:21)*

Does baptism save us by the death of Jesus Christ? No, says Peter. It saves us by the *resurrection* of Jesus Christ.

So again, the resurrection of Christ is directly associated with our salvation. He was killed through our sin — as a direct consequence of sin — but God raised him to life to save us. He was raised to justify us, to make us free. Baptism saves us through the resurrection of Jesus Christ. Without that resurrection, we are still in our sins.

All of these passages have a common thread. If Jesus had stayed dead, there would be no salvation, no forgiveness of sins. Instead, they say that the power of salvation comes from his resurrection.

How does this work? In what way does power come from the resurrection? Should we start looking for a legal principle or an alternative transaction associated with resurrection?

I think that would be a mistake.

Our salvation

Here's a longer passage about salvation in Paul's letter to Titus. As you read this account, note which aspects Paul chooses to emphasize, and which don't even get a mention here.

> *At one time we too were foolish, disobedient, deceived and enslaved by all kinds of passions and pleasures. We lived in malice and envy, being hated and hating one another. But when the kindness and love of God our Savior appeared, he saved us, not because of righteous things we had done, but because of his mercy.*
>
> *He saved us through the washing of rebirth and renewal by the Holy Spirit, whom he poured out on us generously through Jesus Christ our Savior, so that, having been justified by his grace, we might become heirs having the hope of eternal life. This is a trustworthy saying. And I want you to stress these things, so that those who have trusted in God may be careful to devote themselves to doing what is good. These things are excellent and profitable for everyone. (Titus 3:3-8)*

Perhaps pause at this point, and list the points Paul makes. What did you notice?

Here's a quick list: we used to be destructive; through kindness and love God saved us; it was an act of mercy and not something we earned; it involved renewal; the holy spirit is poured on us generously through Jesus; and we are heirs of eternal life.

Now here's a point to notice: even though Paul is describing the process of our salvation in some detail, *he doesn't mention Jesus' death!*

If salvation occurred through a transactional process, then this would be inexplicable. Paul couldn't have left out the one absolutely critical step. On the other hand, if the work of salvation is a process of transformation, a process in which we are changed, then this list is exactly what we would expect.

I think it is very instructive.

Now, please don't infer from any of this that Jesus' death is not important. The emphasis we have placed on the resurrection throughout this whole chapter is not intended to deny the impact or significance of his death. Given Paul's other writings, it is clear that he is totally in awe of Golgotha. The only point I am trying to make is that his death is not the sole fulcrum on which our salvation hinges. His resurrection, in particular, is equally important.

In future sections we will see that the role of Christ's resurrection is quite simple: we need a living Lord! We cannot succeed with a dead Jesus. We need a savior who works in our lives day by day as our mentor, our high priest and guide. Christ died because of me. Now, he lives for me.

As Jesus himself says on the night he was betrayed:

> *Before long the world will not see me any more, but you will see me. Because I live, you also will live. (John 14:19)*

It is not, "Because I die, you will live." It is, "Because I *live*, you also will live."

I am deeply moved at the simplicity of these words. They are just so beautiful.

Summary

If Jesus had stayed dead, then we would still be in our sins. He was raised from the dead by his Father so that we too might walk in newness of life. We are rescued through his resurrection, because we need a living Lord.

Discussion

1. Look again at each of the verses quoted in this chapter. Discuss what implications you understand from them.
2. How does your understanding of salvation change seeing Christ's resurrection as an integral part of the process?
3. Read Acts 17:31. Discuss how the resurrection of Jesus could provide evidence that God has set a day in which Jesus will be the judge of the world.
4. Read the following passage from Romans together:

   Or don't you know that all of us who were baptized into Christ Jesus were baptized into his death? We were therefore buried with him through baptism into death in order that, just as Christ was raised from the dead through the glory of the Father, we too may live a new life.

If we have been united with him like this in his death, we will certainly also be united with him in his resurrection. For we know that our old self was crucified with him so that the body of sin might be done away with, that we should no longer be slaves to sin — because anyone who has died has been freed from sin.

Now if we died with Christ, we believe that we will also live with him. For we know that since Christ was raised from the dead, he cannot die again; death no longer has mastery over him. The death he died, he died to sin once for all; but the life he lives, he lives to God.

In the same way, count yourselves dead to sin but alive to God in Christ Jesus. (Rom 6:3-11)

In the light of this passage, discuss how the resurrection of Jesus ties into our baptisms.

Gave his life

Ask yourself what the phrase *he gave his life* means to you. Just pause for a moment.

Do you equate it with Jesus dying? Does *he gave his life* mean *he died*, and that's all? I don't think so.

He gave his life

Jesus gave his *life*. He gave his life in more than just the narrow sense of dying. We're talking about more than just Golgotha here. Jesus gave his life for us — he gave all of it. All thirty-three years of life. He gave the whole of his life to save us.

Think what this means. It wasn't just that Jesus lived a pretty good life, and then in the end God said, "Look, I need a sacrifice from you for me be able to forgive people." That's not what happened at all.

Right from the start, empowered and directed by his Father, Jesus devoted his life to our salvation. His whole life was totally committed to developing his relationship with his Father, reaching out to the disciples and to the people around, rescuing them — and us — by the teachings he was giving, the very words of life. Peter recognized this:

> *Lord, to whom shall we go? You have the words of eternal life! (John 6:68)*

Every aspect of his life was given to saving people like us.

The shepherd and the wolf

Jesus' parable about the good shepherd seems a bit more tightly focused, though, in that it talks explicitly about dying. How should we think about that?

> *I am the good shepherd. The good shepherd lays down his life for the sheep. The hired hand is not the shepherd who owns the sheep. So when he sees the wolf coming, he abandons the sheep and runs away. Then the wolf attacks the flock and scatters it. The man runs away because he is a hired hand and cares nothing for the sheep. I am the good shepherd; I know my sheep and my sheep know me — just as the Father knows me and I know the Father — and I lay down my life for the sheep (John 10:11-15).*

The wolf comes to the sheep pen; the shepherd lays down his life for the sheep. What does that mean?

Maybe when the wolf comes, the shepherd walks out, lies down and lets the wolf eat him?!

Not at all!

Rather, the wolf comes, and the shepherd comes and engages the wolf in battle, even if it costs him his life. The dying is not the purpose of the battle! The dying is the *consequence* of the conflict. You see the distinction? The battle is the critical thing, the battle that goes right to the end whatever the cost. It is not a battle that just goes part way. Not a battle where the shepherd thinks, "Ouch! I got bitten there!" and runs away. Instead, it is a battle in which the wolf is killed with the last ounce of the shepherd's strength. And so the sheep are saved.

The point is not that the shepherd dies passively; the point is that the shepherd is so committed to the battle that he is willing to lay his life on the line to win the victory, and so to save the sheep.

A greater battle

In the case of Jesus, his dying is part of a greater battle. Hebrews uses the symbol of devil as the enemy to fight to the death, but the idea is the same.

> *Since the children have flesh and blood, he too shared in their humanity so that by his death he might destroy him who holds the power of death — that is, the devil, and free those who all their lives were held in slavery by their fear of death. (Heb 2:14)*

As I say, I think that "the devil" here is a metaphor, in this case meaning the force of temptation within Jesus himself. By his death, Jesus destroyed the devil force of sin within himself. That part of him that was just like you and me, that leads us in opposition to God, that part was there within him too. Time after time he struggled with it. Not my will, but yours be done! (Matt 26:39) Again, and again, and again. He was determined to fight this battle until the enemy was destroyed.

And it was!

In Gethsemane and Golgotha he achieved victory over his flesh, his human nature. And now he joins in the battle with each one of us. He works to bring us victory over our flesh, to help us to realize that we don't really want to give in to the forces of sin and iniquity within us. We may fall into sin, but he calls us to say for ourselves, "No!", "Enough!", "Stop!" "I don't want to go down that path!" We echo his words, "Not my will, Father, but yours be done!"

A grain dies

There's another parable back in John 12:24.

> *I tell you the truth, unless a kernel of wheat falls to the ground and dies, it remains only a single seed. But if it dies, it produces many seeds.*

Here's an experiment to try at home. Take a seed, kill it (perhaps by baking it in the oven), plant it in a pot, and wait for a while...

Nothing will happen. Why?

Because it's not the death of the seed that's important, it's the giving of the life of the seed that's important. You put a living seed in the ground and the seed pours out its life into the plant. It gives its life. See the difference? The seed gives up everything for the life of the plant. It dies to itself, as it were, surrendering the existence it used to know as a seed, and in the process is able to produce the many seeds.

The seed does indeed die. But the point is not a dead seed; the point is that the life was given. There's a continuation of life in the transference of life from the seed into the plant. The seed has to be able to give everything into the life of the plant.

So it is with Christ. He was able and willing to give everything he had into the life of other people. Let's consider a practical example of this: the incident with Jairus in Mark 5:21-43.

Giving strength

Here's how I see the story. Jairus appeals to Jesus to come and save his daughter. She's a twelve year-old girl. Those of us who are parents know the agony that Jairus must have been going through, bearing the daily torment of a child on the brink of death. But now, Jesus is coming to save his daughter!

Imagine him daring to hope...

On the way, in the middle of all those hopes and fears, somebody reaches out and touches the edge of Jesus' robe. Jesus, I presume, is already carrying the emotional weight of Jairus' grief and hope, his desperate pleading. Now he feels yet more strength come out of him (Luke 8:46).

He turns around and asks, "Who touched me?" Peter is astonished. What a ridiculous question! The people are surrounding him; they're all touching him! Jesus says: "No, no... Who was it?"

Finally, the woman stands up. Jesus has been calling for an expression of her faith, for her to stand up and say, "It was me." And now she does! In response, Jesus' compassion flows out to her. He tends to her, and encourages her. He assures her that her faith has made her whole. It's not just her physical healing, but his care and tender concern is healing her spirit too.

Meanwhile …!

Have you ever thought of what Jairus must have been doing at this point? He's going crazy! He's beside himself with worry and grief because Jesus has stopped. Jesus was on the way to heal his daughter, and now he has been interrupted. The timing is desperate, absolutely desperate! She is so close to death. His precious little girl.

Then, tragedy!

They hardly get going again when the terrible news comes: it's too late. The delay was too much. It's too late and now she has died. Gone and lost forever. Imagine what that man felt like!

What is Jesus' response?

Jesus finds yet more reserves within himself. Maybe it's reading too much into the record, but we know in other circumstances Jesus is exhausted by his care for others, and I don't think it is excessive to see it here too. He turns to Jairus and gives even more of himself. He reassures Jairus. It's as if he says to him, "My compassion for others will never come at the cost of my compassion for you. I can do an even greater miracle than you thought was possible. Trust me, my friend."

If even healing the woman cost him strength, what was the cost to raise the little girl back from the dead? How much strength did that draw out of him? How much did he have left to give? Yet he was willing to pay the price.

This is just one example of the way Jesus poured out his life to people like us. He gave himself throughout his life. He gave us his life.

Nowhere to lay his head

On another occasion someone said, "I want to follow you!" Jesus said, "Are you sure? Do you know what it would be like to follow me, with nowhere to sleep?" (Luke 9:8) Peter said, "We've left everything to follow you." (Mark 10:28)

If Peter, Andrew, James and John and all the others had indeed left 'everything' to follow Jesus, think how much more Jesus had already left! Everything! He had never had a wife, or children; never had a career; never had a house of his own, or any of the other comforts we crave in this life, not to mention all his inherent rights as son of God. It's hard for us to conceive the complete and utter devotion of our Lord; pouring every aspect of his life into rescuing us from our path of destruction.

I think Jesus had truly exhausted himself by the time he came to Golgotha. In the literal sense I mean. There was nothing left. He had given every part of his life. When Jesus said that Abraham had rejoiced to see his day and was glad, the response was, "You're not yet fifty...! (John 8:56) This to a man in his early thirties! I wonder how old and tired he looked; pouring every ounce of his strength into serving the people around him, into building them up, rescuing them and saving them. By the time he arrived at Golgotha he had already emptied himself. There was next to nothing left.

And having emptied himself, he enacts his final declaration. I give every part of me to you, my Father.

Summary

When the Scriptures say that Jesus gave his life, it means he gave all of it, not just that he died. Because he loved the Father and the people given into his care, Jesus devoted his life to bringing us into life.

Discussion

1. See what other examples you can think of which show Jesus giving his life to the people around him.
2. If Jesus had led a completely normal life — not especially righteous, standard family and job, etc — how would his impact on us be different?
3. Discuss in what way Jesus' death provides a boundary to his life, like a picture frame, a life lived perfectly.
4. What struggles and challenges did Christ battle with through his life?
5. To what extent are we expected to give our lives for other people?

Blood sacrifice

We have discovered that many "transactional" theories of atonement keep placing the need for Christ's death on God, on his supposed limitations, rather than on us and our very real limitations.

Theory	Claim
Ransom	God had to buy us back from the devil who had gained ownership over us
Satisfaction	God's honor was called into question, so he had to reassert it
Substitution	God needed someone to bear the penalty of sin, so that we could be freed

When we are in this mindset, we can move easily to the idea that God required human sacrifice for one reason or another: that to satisfy his prerequisites, God demanded actual, physical, spilled blood. Without a doubt, there are many verses that talk about the blood of Christ. We may unconsciously read ideas into Bible passages that may not really be there. We'll have to be quite careful.

Understanding the shedding of blood

On the face of it, God does seem to require actual blood to be shed to be able to forgive us. Consider, for example, the second half of Hebrews 9:22

> *... without the shedding of blood there is no forgiveness.*

This verse has often been presented as a law of God. I was taught to consider it an *axiom* of scripture that without the shedding of blood there is no forgiveness, as if it were foundational and beyond debate, perhaps even self-evidently true. Shed blood is needed for forgiveness. Fact! So Jesus had to die so that God could forgive.

But wait a moment! Apart from anything else, suggesting that Jesus had to die so that God *could* forgive, suddenly puts the problem back with God. It places the shortcoming with God, because it says he *could not* forgive unless Jesus died.

Actually, though, when we look at the *whole* verse and think about the context, we find that the writer is talking very specifically about the Law, the Law of Moses. Let's read a larger chunk:

> *This is why even the first covenant was not put into effect without blood. When Moses had proclaimed every commandment of the law to all the people, he took the blood of calves, together with water, scarlet wool and branches of hyssop, and sprinkled the scroll and all the people. He said, "This is the blood of the covenant, which God has commanded you to keep."*
>
> *In the same way, he sprinkled with the blood both the tabernacle and everything used in its ceremonies. In fact, the law requires that nearly everything be cleansed with blood, and without the shedding of blood there is no forgiveness. (Heb 9:18-22)*

It seems to me that the writer is not trying to make a statement about all time. His context is the *Law of Moses*. The Law of Moses, he says, requires that nearly everything must be cleansed with blood, and (in the Law) without the shedding of blood there is no forgiveness. Seen this way, it is simply a statement of analysis, an assertion that can be proved or disproved.

And the analysis is spot on. If we go back to the law of Moses and look at the way forgiveness was achieved, then we discover that everything did indeed have to be 'cleansed' by blood. Moreover, in the Law of Moses there was no forgiveness without the shedding of blood. Read the verse again in this light:

> *In fact, the law requires that nearly everything be cleansed with blood, and without the shedding of blood there is no forgiveness. (Heb 9:22)*

Now that we can see the whole of this verse as a statement about the Law of Moses, the pertinent issue for us is how to apply its teaching to the wider work of God. Within the Law, blood was used for cleansing and for forgiveness. What principle does it lead to that helps in understanding the meaning of the blood of Christ?

It is really important to make this distinction, so let's repeat it: as a *literal statement*, Hebrews 9:22 is a commentary on the Law; however, it's *relevance* to us is a matter of interpretation. That's why we have to ask what principle applies outside the structure of the Law of Moses.

Discovering the principle

Why did the Law of Moses require blood to be shed before God would forgive? We don't have space here for a detailed explanation, but here are some ideas.

First, note that the Law was a system of many symbols, all working together to construct a larger narrative out of the ritual. As the priest or everyday Israelite participated in the symbolic acts, they would be reminded of the narrative. In the days before printed text, the physical acts would remind them about God, and sin, and forgiveness, and life. The foundation of their religion would be right in front of them, present before their hands and eyes, rather like ours is when we immerse ourselves in the words of the Bible.

Second, blood was a significant part of this language of symbols. Theirs was an agricultural community which experienced birth and death with an explicitness that our modern society hides from us. They would help animals birth, and they would slaughter them for their meat and other parts. These are messy processes, with much blood. Powerfully, the Law regulated these occasions to teach religious lessons, by identifying blood with *life*.

> *Be sure you do not eat the blood because the blood is the life and you must not eat the life with the meat. (Deut 12:23)*

In the Law, blood — the literal blood — is the symbol of life; the life of the animal, the life of the human. In fact, this symbolism was already well established by the time Moses gave the Law; it derives from Noah's time:

> *But you must not eat meat that has its lifeblood still in it. And for your lifeblood I will surely demand an accounting. I will demand an accounting from every animal. And from each man, too, I will demand an accounting for the life of his fellow man. "Whoever*

sheds the blood of man, by man shall his blood be shed; for in the image of God has God made man." (Gen 9:4)

Using the interpretation that blood represents life, we can determine the principle behind the phrase, *without the shedding of blood there is no forgiveness*. It is *without the giving of life there is no forgiveness.* As the Israelites spilled the blood of their animals, they would be reminded of their own need to offer their own lives in dedication to God.

So with Jesus. We've already seen what it meant for Jesus to give his life. It wasn't just that he died on Golgotha. Rather, he gave the *whole* of his life to the work God had entrusted to him. He gave it all to guiding other people — us — to life.

And as Jesus devoted his life, so we must devote ours. As he himself says:

Anyone who does not take his cross and follow me is not worthy of me. (Matt 10:38)

For whoever wants to save his life will lose it, but whoever loses his life for me will save it. (Luke 9:24)

But what does "take his cross" or "lose his life" mean in practice? For Jesus it ultimately meant literally losing his life, on the cross. It may too for some of us, but for most of us I don't think it necessarily means physical danger. I suspect it means something like "putting at risk". We are called to put everything we have, and all that we are, at risk: our jobs, our money, our friends, our selves, even our families. That doesn't mean giving them all up, but being willing to give them up.

Jesus is quite blunt. Offer your life, all of it, to the deepest service of God, and then you will truly find life. Otherwise, you will lose it.

Forgiveness does not take place without the giving of your life.

Cleanse our conscience

The writer to the Hebrews makes a similar point earlier in the same chapter we have been considering.

The blood of goats and bulls and the ashes of a heifer sprinkled on those who are ceremonially unclean sanctify them so that they are outwardly clean. How much more, then, will the blood of Christ, who through the eternal Spirit offered himself unblemished to God,

> *cleanse our consciences from acts that lead to death, so that we may serve the living God! (Heb 9:13-14)*

Did you notice? The role of Christ's sacrifice is to *cleanse our consciences.* It's not about getting God to agree with us, nor about appeasing God. Rather it is about affecting the mind, the conscience, the attitude and the heart of the person bringing the sacrifice, and perhaps of those looking on too.

As we'll continue to see over the next few sections, this was actually the point about the sacrifices under the Law also. They were supposed to affect the one who offered them. And if the sacrifices of the Law had that effect on the people who witnessed them, just think how much more effective the blood of Christ is to us who witness his sacrifice again and again as we read Scripture, or as we share bread and wine in communion. His spilled blood has incredible power in cleansing our consciences from acts that lead to death.

Summary

Blood is a symbol of life, so blood sacrifices were symbolically about the giving of life. God wants us to be like Jesus and each to be willing to give up every aspect of our life so that we might truly find it.

Discussion

1. If God didn't really need spilled blood, why do you think it is so prevalent in the Law of Moses?
2. What do you think 'without the giving of life, there is no forgiveness' might mean in practice? Discuss in what ways you have each "given your life".
3. What is the difference between obedience, submission, turning the other cheek, etc, and being a doormat?

Mercy, not appeasement

Another reason that people feel led to believe a substitutionary theory of atonement is that some Bible passages concerning *propitiation* can appear to support that theory pretty explicitly. But I believe this is due to a mistranslation of the authors' intent. In this section I'd like us to examine this sacrifice word which appears in various versions of our English Bibles. Take this verse in the KJV translation, for example:

> *And he is the propitiation for our sins: and not for ours only, but also for the sins of the whole world. (1 John 2:2, KJV)*

Because propitiation is a word we don't use day to day, it can escape our scrutiny. We may not be very familiar with its actual meaning. But a trip to the dictionary will fix that. The dictionary on my computer has a definition as follows.

> *Propitiate: Win or regain the favor of (a god, spirit, or person) by doing something that pleases them :* the pagans thought it was important to propitiate the gods with sacrifices.
>
> *Propitiation: The act of propitiating or appeasing a god, spirit, or person :* he lifted his hands in propitiation.

Propitiation or appeasement happens when someone tries to find a way to pacify another, to give them a gift, for example. Perhaps a parent is furious with a child, and the child tries to find some way to make the parent happier, "Would you like me to give you something?" with the unspoken, "to make you less angry with me."

Is this really our relationship with God?

Remember that the Bible wasn't originally written in English. The New Testament was written in Common Greek, a language that faded from use over a thousand years ago, so our English Bibles come from the very hard work of many diligent people, translating from an ancient tongue into our modern vernacular. It's not at all an automatic process, but rather it involves thoughtful consideration and careful judgment. Unfortunately, despite their best intentions, the beliefs and doctrines of the translators have affected their choice of words within the translation.

I think this has happened with *propitiation.* I'll risk being bold here: in my opinion, the choice of the word *propitiation* is such a poor translation that it should be crossed out and replaced with something more representative of what the original writers intended.

Propitiation is very much a substitution-theory kind of word. That's why it was a popular choice in King James' time when the KJV was translated, and it is still the word of choice for some modern translators.

But *propitiation* is manipulative: it seeks to distract or divert God's attention by doing something that pleases him. Yet God is not to be manipulated. Nor is he in turn manipulative of us. The death of Christ is not about appeasement. God has never needed to calm down, or to get over something.

In fact, the Biblical picture of our relationship with God is completely the other way around. It is that God is reaching out to us, wanting a response. The picture we should have in our minds is of a parent 'disciple-ing' a child in the context of overwhelming love; *disciplining* a child in the rich sense of that word: training a child.

What the Greek words mean

To understand the original ideas a little better let's dip into the Greek. The original family of Greek words that *propitiation* supposedly translates are *hilaskomai*, *hilasterion*, and *hilasmos*. Each of these words occurs just twice in the New Testament. You can see that they all have the same stem (*hilas*-) but also that they reflect different parts of speech, just like 'walk', 'walking' and 'walked', for example. We'll look at all six occurrences of these words in the New Testament, to see the pattern of their meaning.

1st occurrence

Five of the uses of *hilas*- words are in the context of atonement, so we risk getting into a circular argument by going there. Interestingly, one of the occurrences is in a completely different context. It is a parable of Jesus: the parable of the Pharisee and the tax collector.

> *To some who were confident of their own righteousness and looked down on everybody else, Jesus told this parable: "Two men went up to the temple to pray, one a Pharisee and the other a tax collector. The Pharisee stood up and prayed about himself: 'God, I thank you that I am not like other men — robbers, evildoers, adulterers — or even like this tax collector. I fast twice a week and give a tenth of all I get.'*
>
> *"But the tax collector stood at a distance. He would not even look up to heaven, but beat his breast and said, 'God, have mercy on me, a sinner.'*
>
> *"I tell you that this man, rather than the other, went home justified before God. For everyone who exalts himself will be humbled, and he who humbles himself will be exalted." (Luke 18:9-14)*

The Pharisee comes and prays 'about' (or possibly 'with') himself, "I thank you that I am not like other men, especially not like this tax collector!" and he goes on to list the marvelous things he does for God.

The tax collector, in contrast, comes to God and prays, asking God to be merciful to him, a sinner.

In the original, this word 'merciful' is *hilaskomai*!

Doesn't that show us how far off the translation 'propitiation' is? *Hilaskomai* is not about appeasement. It's about mercy. "God, there's no reason why you have to accept me. I just throw myself on your mercy." That's the whole point of the parable. The Pharisee is the one saying, "I'm doing everything you wanted me to do! You should be pleased!" *He's* the one trying to be propitious. In contrast, the tax collector says, "I throw myself on your mercy! Will you accept me?"

2nd occurrence

The other occurrence of *hilaskomai* is in Hebrews. This is how the NIV translates it:

> *For this reason he had to be made like his brothers in every way, in order that he might become a merciful and faithful high priest in service to God, and that he might make atonement for the sins of the people (Heb 2:17).*

The NIV translators picked the phrase *make atonement*, which is okay but could sound transactional if we were not careful. Now try rereading the verse and substitute the plain idea of *mercy* instead of a transaction for *atonement*:

> *For this reason he had to be made like his brothers in every way, in order that he might become a merciful and faithful high priest in service to God, and that he might have mercy for the sins of the people.*

It can be translated in exactly the same way as in Luke! Incidentally, while *hilaskomai* has the idea of mercy in the sense of pardoning or forgiving, the other word that is translated merciful in this verse has more the idea of empathy. Thus Jesus is an empathetic and faithful high priest, who pardons our sins.

3rd occurrence

Let's move to another of our family of words, *hilasterion.* It occurs in Romans 3. Here it is in the KJV translation:

> *Whom God hath set forth to be a propitiation through faith in his blood, to declare his righteousness for the remission of sins that are past, through the forbearance of God; (Rom 3:25, KJV)*

There's the use of the word *propitiation.* The King James translators chose this word in 1611 as a translation of *hilasterion.* The NIV avoids *propitiation*, and instead uses the phrase *sacrifice of atonement*, which still feels very transactional, at least to me.

The *Diaglott*[*] interlinear translation of the Greek text takes issue with *propitiation,* and extends the understanding of 'mercy' to *hilasterion,* too. Here is the Diaglott's translation of Romans 3:25. This is a word for word translation of the Greek text, keeping the same word order of the original:

> *... whom set forth the God a mercy-seat through the faith by the of him blood, for a pointing out of the righteousness of himself, through the passing by of the formerly committed sins in the forbearance of the God.*

---

* *The Emphatic Diaglott, Kessinger Publishing LLC, 2006.*

The word *hilasterion* is translated mercy-*seat*. Jesus is the mercy-seat, the place where mercy is obtained. The footnote to this verse in the *Diaglott* goes on to assert that *"hilasterion never signifies propitiation,"* and that it is always used to express the mercy seat.

4th occurrence

Indeed, the other occurrence of *hilasterion* is clearly of this nature:

> *Above the ark were the cherubim of the Glory, overshadowing the atonement cover. (Heb 9:5)*

Notice that while the NIV uses the phrase *atonement cover*, the KJV and others use *mercy seat*:

> *And over it the cherubims of glory shadowing the mercyseat; of which we cannot now speak particularly. (KJV)*

Either way, the same idea is intended. *Hilasterion* is the top of the covenant box built by Moses, which had a seat that represented God's throne. This is the place where the Israelites came to meet with God, and hence receive mercy. It was from here that God dispensed his compassionate justice.

Notice that both the KJV and the NIV agree that, here at least, *hilasterion* is not propitiation, nor even *atoning sacrifice.*

5th and 6th occurrences

Exactly the same kind of idea comes across with the final word, *hilasmos*, which occurs twice in John's first letter. Here it is in the NIV:

> *He is the atoning sacrifice for our sins, and not only for ours but also for the sins of the whole world. (1 John 2:2)*

> *This is love: not that we loved God, but that he loved us and sent his Son as an atoning sacrifice for our sins. (1 John 4:10)*

The NIV uses the idea of atoning sacrifice again, as it did with one of the occurrences of each of the other two words (though not with the other occurrences). The KJV uses *propitiation* in both verses. For example:

> *Herein is love, not that we loved God, but that he loved us, and sent his Son to be the propitiation for our sins. (KJV)*

However, the Greek Lexicon by Louw and Nida* objects to this translation. They state:

> *Though some traditional translations render hilasterion as 'propitiation,' this involves a wrong interpretation of the term in question. Propitiation is essentially a process by which one does a favor to a person in order to make him or her favorably disposed, but in the NT God is never the object of propitiation since he is already on the side of people. Hilasmos and hilasterion denote the means of forgiveness and not propitiation.*

In fact, these verses make perfect sense if we simply translate *hilasmos* with the idea of merciful forgiveness. Then they are simply expressing the idea of God's mercy towards us, and we can abandon any idea of appeasement.

> *He is the [means of mercy] for our sins, and not only for ours but also for the sins of the whole world.*

> *This is love: not that we loved God, but that he loved us and sent his Son as a [means of mercy] for our sins.*

Jesus brings mercy. He is the place of mercy. He is the one who is merciful. His role is not to placate God. That would suggest that his work is to get God to do something different, that the problem is with God. Quite the reverse. The problem is with us, and God sent him to us to bring us mercy.

Propitiation should be taken out of our vocabulary!

Summary

The technical English word 'propitiation' (appeasement) is often used to describe the purpose of the death of Jesus. But it is a mistranslation of a family of words in the original of the New Testament. Rather, the idea behind these words is merciful forgiveness, not appeasement.

---

* *Louw & Nida, Greek-English Lexicon of the New Testament: Based on Semantic Domains, United Bible Societies, 1988.*

Discussion

1. In practice, what is the difference between the ideas of mercy and appeasement? Invent a story or parable that exemplifies each one.
2. Discuss in what ways translators' biases can either be helpful or harmful in understanding the Bible. Can you think of some specific examples?
3. Consider the following verse from Leviticus,

   For the life of a creature is in the blood, and I have given it to you to make atonement for yourselves on the altar; it is the blood that makes atonement for one's life. (Lev 17:11)

   Discuss whether it can be interpreted in accordance with the approach in this chapter.

Covering

Have you ever heard the phrase "Jesus is a covering for sin"? It is a popular expression. Martin Luther expressed the concept saying we are *covered by the righteousness of Christ*. I've heard this linked with the idea that *God cannot look on sin,* which I presume is drawn from Habbakuk. *Covering* is another place in which some Christians think that the death of Christ was intended to change something in heaven, so that God could accept us. So let's look at this idea carefully.

In what sense can it be said that God cannot look on sin?

Perhaps God looks at me and sees a sinner, but then he covers me with Christ in some way and so imagines I'm not that bad after all? Almost like a game of pretend.

Clearly not. God doesn't play games with himself. So there must be another way to look at this.

Similarly, popular interpretations of a passage in Genesis say that it was for God's own sake that he provided a covering of skins for Adam and Eve.

Adam and Eve had attempted to cover themselves with fig leaves, but instead God makes clothing of animal skins for them. I've heard many people suggest that God took a lamb and slew it to provide Adam and Eve with their clothing, that this was the first blood sacrifice, and that God is showing that the literal shedding of blood is necessary to cover sins. But that's going way beyond what the Bible says.

> *The LORD God made garments of skin for Adam and his wife and clothed them. (Gen 3:21)*

That's all it says!

It doesn't say it was a sheep. Perhaps it was. Or perhaps it was a lion, or bear. It doesn't even say that God killed it. Maybe he did, or maybe it had died previously.

All I'm suggesting is that we should be really careful about reading more into a passage than is written. Sometimes it's valid and, no doubt, sometimes it's not.

In this case, going with the popular interpretation can get us into trouble. Why? Because it is confused about where the shortcoming is. It says that God is the one who needs us to be covered. It says that the problem is with God, that he is not able to accept us the way we are, and so God has to invent the idea of a 'covering' to resolve his issue!

This is not good. As we have been noticing, the real problem is with us. It is always with us. It is never with God.

Our fear and shame

Who actually needs a covering? Or to put it another way, who would have the problem if we came to God (spiritually) naked? God, or us?

I think the answer is that we do. I don't think *God* needs us to be "covered". He knows exactly who we are, and what we are like. Rather, we are the ones who feel a desperate need for covering. Here's why.

When we come face-to-face with God, we have natural and understandable reactions: we feel ashamed, we are afraid, we hide.

We're ashamed because we aspire to be so much better than we are, to be so much more than we have accomplished. We're afraid because God is so awesome and we are so weak and frail; he could destroy us in a moment. And then shame and terror manifest themselves in a reaction to hide.

Consider what Adam and Eve did. They took the fruit; suddenly their eyes were opened and they realized they were naked. They had been naked all along, but suddenly they realize how totally naked they are before God. Spiritually naked, as well as physically. They feel the awful shame of inadequacy.

Their reaction was immediate: they covered themselves with whatever was handy. They picked fig leaves and joined them together in a rudimentary covering, attempting to hide their fear and shame. They suddenly saw their literal nakedness as representing their spiritual nakedness, and wanted to do something about it. This was the best they could come up with.

Then they heard the voice of the LORD God, walking in the garden in the cool of the evening.

What was their response to the sound of God?

They hid! Even though they had tried to cover themselves, they still hid. Why? Because they still felt naked. Within themselves they knew that they were afraid of God; afraid of his presence.

So they hid.

Their shame separated them from God.

Overcoming fear and shame

There are many other places in the Bible where people experience fear in the presence of God. Just think, almost the first thing Gabriel says to Mary is, "Don't be afraid." (Luke 1:30) In fact, the angels seems to spend much of their time trying to reassure people, encouraging them not to be afraid! We fall into mortal dread when confronted by the divine.

Isaiah 6 is particularly instructive.

Isaiah is drawn into a vision of heaven. Like Paul later, he probably had no idea whether he was bodily in heaven or simply in a vision, but either way he experiences the presence of God. He sees God seated on his high throne, with glorious seraphim around him declaring, "Holy, holy, holy..."

And Isaiah is overcome with dread.

> *'Woe to me!' I cried. 'I am ruined! For I am a man of unclean lips, and I live among a people of unclean lips, and my eyes have seen the King, the LORD Almighty' (Is 6:5).*

This is our natural state when confronted with the majesty and awesome glory of God. Fear, and dread. So what happens next?

> *Then one of the seraphs flew to me with a live coal in his hand, which he had taken with tongs from the altar. With it he touched my*

> *mouth and said, 'See, this has touched your lips; your guilt is taken away and your sin atoned for' (Is 6:6-7).*

Even in a vision, I imagine Isaiah feels a brief searing pain. Unclean lips, now cauterized by fire from the altar.

But hang on! Atonement by burning your lips? What's going on here? Why would God need Isaiah's lips to be burned? Where in Scripture is the doctrine of atonement through literal burning by fire?

Nowhere, of course! There is no Biblical doctrine of atonement with hot coals* on the lips. So, what's going on here?

The text doesn't explain it, so it's hard to be definitive. But consider this: Isaiah is terrified; he is truly aware of his weakness and his limitations. Isaiah knows very well the lying and cheating rampant in his community, and is equally conscious of his own imperfections too. Untamable tongue! Unclean lips!

So it is his lips that the seraph scorches with fire. This is a symbolic act designed to say, "I have dealt with your problem. You no longer need to worry about feeling unworthy!"

It's a powerful physical statement.

Look at the effect this symbolic act has on Isaiah. It fills him with reassurance. It transforms him! One minute he is, "Woe to me! I am ruined! I am a man of unclean lips." The next minute?

> *Then I heard the voice of the Lord saying, 'Whom shall I send? And who will go for us?" And I said, 'Here am I. Send me!' (Is 6:8)*

Do you see what that live coal did? It took the fearful Isaiah, terrified at the presence of God, and transformed him into a prophet who stands up straight, who is willing to go out as God's messenger! If you read the rest of the chapter, you'll see that it transforms him into an ambassador for God, ready to go out and preach and preach and preach, whether the people are prepared to listen or not. For how long? Until the cities lie ruined without inhabitant and the houses are left deserted, the fields ruined and ravaged, until there's no possibility of doing anything more.

---

* *There is a* metaphor *in Scripture about being refined by fire (e.g. Zech 13:9), but that's quite different from Isaiah's experience.*

These live coals are God's object-lesson, a parable for Isaiah to experience to help him, to give him courage and confidence.

Interpreting the skins

I think the same kind of thing took place with Adam and Eve. It could have been *they* who considered their fig leaves inadequate, not God. Now Scripture is not explicit on this point, so whichever viewpoint we might hold will be a matter of interpretation. But note this: the very fact that Adam and Eve hid, provides strong evidence that they found their fig leaf clothing inadequate. Even though they had a kind of covering, they still felt naked. They were still afraid of God, and in their fear they hid.

This is not what God wants. He doesn't want us to shrink back and hide from him. As the New Testament says,

> *But we are not of those who shrink back and are destroyed, but of those who believe and are saved. (Heb 10:39)*

So what does God do? He provides them with a better covering so that they will feel confident about coming back into his presence. He takes the skins of an animal, and makes clothes for them.

I'm not sure in what sense the skins were better for Adam and Eve than the fig leaves. It might have been a physical improvement, in that they were more sturdy and less likely to tear. Or there might have been a symbolic element like with Isaiah, a sense that God had done something so that they need not be so worried. Either way, it seems that God provided them skins to encourage them out of the bushes and back into his presence.

Over time, God is successful in drawing them back. After being banished from the garden, they do indeed have the courage to approach God again.

Confidence

Back to confidence: the same theme lies behind some of the arguments advanced by the writer to the Hebrews. The work of Christ is intended to give us confidence, just like the work of the angels back in Eden, or the work of the seraph in Isaiah. The work of Jesus is to give us courage, to have us stand up, to have us be willing to come near to God.

> *Therefore, since we have a great high priest who has gone through the heavens, Jesus the Son of God, let us hold firmly to the faith we profess. For we do not have a high priest who is unable to sympathize with our weaknesses, but we have one who has been tempted in every way, just as we are — yet was without sin. Let us then approach the throne of grace with confidence, so that we may receive mercy and find grace to help us in our time of need (Heb 4:14-16).*

Approach the throne of grace with confidence! God doesn't want us to hide in the bushes. He wants us to stand up and be sure of our reception as we approach his throne.

Now let's be clear. This is not the sort of confidence that says, "Here I am, God, I'm perfect and ready..." That was the attitude of the Pharisee in Jesus' parable in Luke 18. Rather, it's a kind of confidence that enables us to say, "Here I am. I am ready to serve. You have picked me up, you have made me new. I'm your servant and despite my failings, I know you love me. I'm ready for you to send me out. How do you want me to serve?"

Underlying this attitude is the assurance that we're not going to be turned away. When we need something from God, when we're in our time of need, he wants us to approach with confidence.

God is reaching out to us. He has proved it by not sparing his own son. Do you want any greater proof that God already loves you? How much more could he possibly do to encourage you to come to him? If he did not spare his only son, will he not also generously give you everything you need?

We learn a major principle of salvation here: God works to reassure us. Almost every thing God does, one way or another, is him reaching out. "Let me give you courage, let me give you strength, let me give you an idea of the love I have for you."

So let us truly have a sense of courage and confidence to approach the throne of grace, so that we may receive mercy and find grace to help us in our time of need.

Summary

When God provides a covering, he does it for our sake, as a way to give us confidence; from the first literal covering of Adam and Eve, through to the symbolic covering of Christ. He does so to help us overcome our fear and shame, so that we may have courage in coming to his throne of grace.

Discussion

1. What benefits could God derive from us being covered? Now consider what benefits we could derive from being covered. Which ones are more convincing?
2. Discuss why the Bible uses physical nakedness as a metaphor for spiritual shortcomings (e.g. in Rev 3:17).
3. Habbakuk says, "Your eyes are too pure to look on evil." (Hab 1:13) This phrase could mean many things. Look at the context of the verse. What does Habbakuk mean when he says this?

Law and Christ

What is the relationship between the Law of Moses and the work of Christ? Getting this mixed up can lead to all sorts of confusion. So in this section, we'll tackle the question of how they relate, and specifically what we should expect to learn from the one about the other.

The Law of Moses

God gave the Law of Moses to the people of Israel to provide national governance when Israel was liberated from mass slavery. As a people, Israel was shifting from a patriarchal family culture into a multi-tribal nation, and the Law was designed to provide social, moral, and spiritual infrastructure.

This was all 1500 years before Jesus came. That fact alone can create complications for us when we think about the relationship between Christ and the Law.

Because the Law came first in time, we might treat the Law as if it was something fundamental, and Christ merely as the fulfillment of this Law. "If only we could understand the Law properly," we might say, "then we'd be able to understand Christ." I've heard many Christians make this claim.

But this is backward!

According to the New Testament, *Christ* is the fundamental truth, the ultimate revelation. He stands in his own right. It is *Christ* who is the embodiment of everything God wants to say to us. Salvation from God has always been focused in Christ.

This is how Paul puts it:

> *And he made known to us the mystery of his will according to his good pleasure, which he purposed in Christ, to be put into effect*

> *when the times will have reached their fulfillment — to bring all things in heaven and on earth together under one head, even Christ. (Eph 1:9-10)*

> *[God] who has saved us and called us to a holy life — not because of anything we have done but because of his own purpose and grace. This grace was given us in Christ Jesus before the beginning of time, but it has now been revealed through the appearing of our Savior, Christ Jesus, who has destroyed death and has brought life and immortality to light through the gospel. (2 Tim 1:9-10)*

Even before Adam and Eve were made, God had his son in mind. In fact, God had his *glorified* son in mind. God knew what agony he would ask of Jesus:

> *... the Lamb that was slain from the creation of the world. (Rev 13:8)*

and he knew the glory he would fulfill in Jesus ...

> *I have brought you glory on earth by completing the work you gave me to do. And now, Father, glorify me in your presence with the glory I had with you before the world began. (John 17:4-5)*

Jesus looks for the reassurance that comes from that glory as he goes through his agony, as he goes to submit himself completely to God.

The point is that God designed salvation around Christ right from the start. Here's the principle he states in Isaiah:

> *I make known the end from the beginning, from ancient times, what is still to come. I say: My purpose will stand, and I will do all that I please. (Is 46:10)*

The Law is a shadow

So, if Jesus comes first in God's plan, how should we think about the symbols in the Law? What was really going on at Passover? What was the ritual of the Red Heifer all about? Or the Scapegoat? Or in any other component of the Law such as the Tabernacle?

> *These are a shadow of the things that were to come; the reality, however, is found in Christ. (Col 2:17)*

All of the requirements and procedures of the Law of Moses were a shadow of another reality; all of them were merely dim reflections of a more fundamental truth.

Christ is the fundamental truth. The Law is a collection of shadows cast on the wall.

So we have a choice. We could look at shadows on a wall and try to figure out what the primary object is like, or we could look at the primary object directly and then better understand why the shadows look the way they do. The second is clearly more sensible.

Indeed, it is when we understand Christ in all his three-dimensional full-color glory, that we will be best suited to go back to study the Law, to explore and understand the various aspects of it.

Take the tabernacle, for example.

> *They serve at a sanctuary that is a copy and shadow of what is in heaven. This is why Moses was warned when he was about to build the tabernacle: "See to it that you make everything according to the pattern shown you on the mountain." (Heb 8:5)*

The tabernacle was simply a pale imitation of what Moses saw when he went up on the mount and saw the Temple of God, there, in heaven! He saw God on a throne (Ex 24:9-11), with presumably the four living creatures around, the angels and the seraphim, the cherubim — all the other elements of heaven that we learn from Isaiah, Ezekiel, and Revelation — and God said to Moses, "I want you to make a tent which depicts this!" So Moses went back, and he did just that. He worked with others who were also given particular skills and capabilities by the spirit of God, and he made a tent that depicted God's reality in heaven.

God did not mold the reality in heaven on the tent Moses made on earth. No! It's the other way round. The reality is in heaven, the tent depicted it.

Entering the tabernacle in heaven

When Christ ascended to take on his role as high priest, he participated in the reality that is in heaven. He did not participate in the shadow, or the reflection that had been constructed here on earth. This is how the writer to the Hebrews describes it:

When Christ came as high priest of the good things that are already here, he went through the greater and more perfect tabernacle that is not man-made, that is to say, not a part of this creation. (Heb 9:11)

From the foundation of the world, God saw this fundamental act. Christ entered the most holy place in heaven, bearing a gift of his blood, his life. The triumph of Christ *is* that he was slain and rose again. More, that he was *willing* to be slain, trusting that God would indeed raise him up. As he says,

No one takes [my life] from me, but I lay it down of my own accord. I have authority to lay it down and authority to take it up again. This command I received from my Father." (John 10:18)

Paul says it this way,

And being found in appearance as a man, he humbled himself and became obedient to death — even death on a cross! (Phil 2:8)

So Jesus enters heaven, bearing the marks of his submission. His blood is symbolic of the fact that he had completely devoted every part of his life to his Father. Here is my life, and I give it to you.

The nature of sacrifice

What Christ did is the reality. The Law, and other parts of the Old Testament, are the shadows of this reality. Again, once we understand Christ, then we will better see the same principles reflected in the Law.

The reality is Christ, offering his life in sacrifice to God. He gave the whole of his life, both while living and while dying; total devotion and commitment to the path of eternity. And having seen the reality in Christ, we find that the Old Testament teaching of sacrifice is completely consistent.

First, *God* has no need for humans to give him animal flesh:

I have no need of a bull from your stall or of goats from your pens, for every animal of the forest is mine, and the cattle on a thousand hills. (Ps 50:9-10)

Or again,

> *You do not delight in sacrifice, or I would bring it; you do not take pleasure in burnt offerings. (Ps 51:16)*

so the lamb isn't offered for God's benefit.

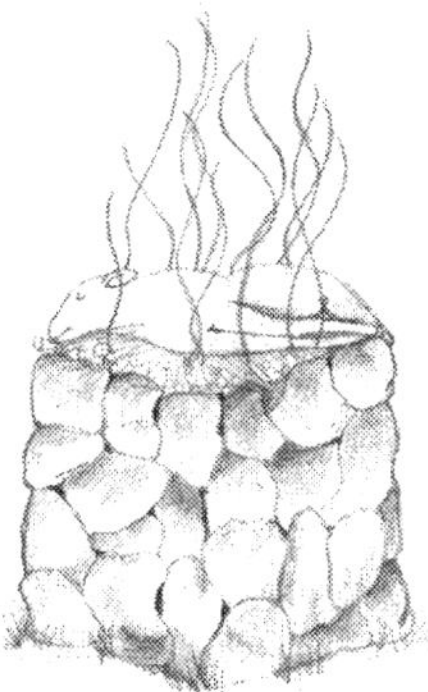

Second, sacrifice was never "doing a deal" with God. The life of a lamb was not offered *instead* of the life of the sinner. Rather, the life of the lamb was supposed to remind the offerer that his or her life also belonged to God, and needed to be offered and devoted to God. Here's a stunning and definitive scripture given through Micah,

> *With what shall I come before the LORD and bow down before the exalted God? Shall I come before him with burnt offerings, with calves a year old? Will the LORD be pleased with thousands of rams, with ten thousand rivers of oil? Shall I offer my firstborn for my transgression, the fruit of my body for the sin of my soul? He has showed you, O man, what is good. And what does the LORD require of you? To act justly and to love mercy and to walk humbly with your God. (Mic 6:8)*

The sacrifices, presenting dead animals, that's not what God wants! The big gifts, the rivers of oil — "I could pour them out..." — that's not what God wants! Shall I take my son and kill him? God would be appalled!

No! says Micah. God doesn't want any of those things. He wants your heart! He wants you to act justly, to love mercy, and to walk humbly with your God.

Summary

The Law of Moses is a shadow of the realities found in Christ. He is the original, the Law is the derivation. In particular, taking his own life-blood as the offering, Jesus entered the real tabernacle in heaven, an event which the Old Testament imagery was designed to represent.

Discussion

1. To what extent does God know the future before it happens? Suggest some examples from everyday life.
2. How does the approach of this section apply to understanding prophecy? Think about what it says about Judas, for example.
3. In what way does your understanding of the Law of Moses change if you think of it as shadows of Christ cast back in time?

Salvation before Christ

With what we learned in the last section, we can go further, and explore the nature of salvation in the Old Testament. Here's a question that I've heard people debate over the years:

Has the 'mechanism' of salvation changed with the death of Christ?

On the one hand, this question might seem purely academic. After all, surely I don't really care how Abraham or Joshua or Isaiah was saved! God knows, and while I might be curious, it has no direct impact on my life.

But on the other hand, by exploring how Abraham or Joshua or Isaiah was saved, I might, in turn, learn something about how we are saved. And that's something that does have a direct impact on my life.

Has the mechanism of salvation changed?

I know some Christians who hold a doctrine that says there have been a number of distinct dispensations, and that the mechanism of salvation in one period was not the same as in another. According to this doctrine, there was a huge change at the death of Christ. The whole structure of salvation changed. Some Christians even think that yet another epoch started at Pentecost, when the path to salvation shifted again. Each of these epochs may have come with their own mechanisms of salvation, and what was acceptable to God in one, may not be acceptable in another.

Are there really distinct dispensations like this?

Clearly the form of worship changes over time. The nomadic worship of Abraham and Job is quite different from the regularized temple worship of Hezekiah, which in turn is quite different from the collective synagogue worship of the New Testament.

But does the essential purpose change from epoch to epoch? Or to put the question the other way round: has the 'mechanism' of salvation always been the same?

I've heard this question asked in the following way: "Is the sacrifice of Christ effective for those in the Old Testament period?"

Now, to be honest, I never really knew what that question meant. I could never figure out what 'effective' meant in this context. The concept seemed too woolly for me to understand what really was being asked. Or maybe the question had some built-in assumptions about heaven-based transactions that I wasn't ready to accept.

Fortunately, Paul allows us to sidestep the question completely.

Paul's view of Abraham and David

In Romans 3, Paul writes about the salvation that we have in Christ.

> *But now a righteousness from God, apart from law, has been made known, to which the Law and the Prophets testify. This righteousness from God comes through faith in Jesus Christ to all who believe. There is no difference, for all have sinned and fall short of the glory of God, and are justified freely by his grace through the redemption that came by Christ Jesus. (Rom 3:21-24)*

Without a doubt, Paul is describing salvation under Christ. He continues in the same vein right through to the end of Romans 3 and on into to Romans 4, in which he writes,

> *What then shall we say that Abraham, our forefather, discovered in this matter? If, in fact, Abraham was justified by works, he had something to boast about – but not before God. What does the Scripture say? "Abraham believed God, and it was credited to him as righteousness." (Rom 4:1-3)*

Let's just stop there!

Even without going further, the obvious question is, why on earth would Paul look to Abraham if Abraham was saved by a different 'mechanism' than we?! It wouldn't make sense.

Think about the flow of the argument. Paul is talking about salvation, about righteousness, about being justified before God, and he says: "Okay, let's look at Abraham and see what he discovered in this matter," and he goes on to draw parallels between Abraham and us. He describes the way Abraham is saved in order to draw conclusions about our salvation.

Here's the point I'm trying to make: Paul must believe that Abraham was saved in the same way that we are. Do you see?

If Paul believed that a different mechanism of salvation was at work, he would never think of drawing on Abraham's experience to explain how we are saved.

As if that's not enough, Paul goes on to draw a parallel with David too:

> *David says the same thing when he speaks of the blessedness of the man to whom God credits righteousness apart from works.*
> *(Rom 4:6)*

Paul looks at both Abraham and David and says, "These men already understood salvation, and they've been telling us about it. It's part of what the Law and the Prophets have been testifying to."

So, unless we are prepared to disagree with Paul on this matter, we too have to presume that Abraham and David were saved in the same way that we are saved. It wasn't that God had one way to save them, and has come up with a different way to save us. Abraham and David were saved by the same 'mechanism', the same process, by which we are saved.

Incidentally, Paul is not the only New Testament writer to draw this kind of lesson about salvation from the Old Testament. James does too, quoting the same incident about Abraham:

> *You foolish man, do you want evidence that faith without deeds is useless? Was not our ancestor Abraham considered righteous for what he did when he offered his son Isaac on the altar? You see that his faith and his actions were working together, and his faith was made complete by what he did. And the scripture was fulfilled that says, "Abraham believed God, and it was credited to him as righteousness," and he was called God's friend. You see that a person is justified by what he does and not by faith alone.*
> *(Jas 2:20-24)*

Again, James calls on us to learn lessons about the path to salvation by looking at Abraham, which would only make sense if the way of salvation was the same for Abraham as it is for us.

To take a final example: consider the following view expressed by the writer to the Hebrews (the writer is probably Barnabas, but it's hard to be sure).

> *Now faith is being sure of what we hope for and certain of what we do not see. This is what the ancients were commended for [...]*
>
> *These were all commended for their faith, yet none of them received what had been promised. God had planned something better for us so that only together with us would they be made perfect. Therefore, since we are surrounded by such a great cloud of witnesses, let us throw off everything that hinders and the sin that so easily entangles, and let us run with perseverance the race marked out for us. Let us fix our eyes on Jesus, the author and perfecter of our faith, who for the joy set before him endured the cross, scorning its shame, and sat down at the right hand of the throne of God. Consider him who endured such opposition from sinful men, so that you will not grow weary and lose heart. (Heb 11:1-2, 11:39-12:3)*

From these examples, we have to conclude that the New Testament writers considered the process of salvation to be fundamentally unchanged across all times and ages.

Two conclusions

There are a couple of conclusions we can draw from these passages.

The first builds directly on the main point we have been making: that the passages argue against dispensational doctrines, at least at the level of the fundamental path to salvation. According to these authors, the same mechanism of salvation applies across the sweep of revealed history.

Now, if you think about it, you will probably notice that dispensational doctrines and transactional doctrines go hand in hand. If atonement requires that a transaction has to occur in heaven, then there is a time before the transaction, and a time after it, which leads naturally to multiple dispensations. Or to put it the other way around, if there are no distinct dispensations with respect to salvation, then it is unlikely that salvation is fundamentally dependent on a transaction taking place.

We now have another piece of evidence that leads us away from a transactional interpretation of the atonement.

A second conclusion comes from noticing that all these passages relate to *faith.* In Old and New Testaments alike, we find faith as a common thread. If you didn't notice it, just pause and have a quick look at the passages again.

In the Abraham passage, the faith-word is disguised slightly: it's the word "believed". In the Greek it is clearly the same word as faith; it's just that in English it's not considered proper grammar to say, "Abraham faith-ed God ..." Similarly, in the David passage, the idea of faith is there by implication, as a contrast to salvation through works. In the other passages, the faith idea is very explicit.

So what's important about *faith*? Why should God care whether we have faith or not?

At this stage we'll leave it just as a question to mull over. But we will note the following: faith is something that happens in us — it is a change in who we are, it is not a transaction that takes place in heaven.

Summary

The principles for salvation across the Old and New Testaments are the same. Faith was the basis for salvation in the Old Testament, just as it is in the New. While the details of worship may be different, God has always sought to win our hearts and minds.

Discussion

1. Is it more reasonable that the route to salvation has been the same through the ages, or that a different route exists in each era?
2. What do you think Abraham and David might have known about Jesus? What about the average Israelite?
3. What was sacrifice for? Do you think it succeeded in it's purpose?
4. Why do you think God has always looked for faith? What does faith accomplish or enable?

The purpose of God

So, how are we saved? What is the mechanism used by God? What is the process?

We have spent a lot of time arguing that the mechanism of salvation is not a transaction that takes place in heaven, but rather that it's about a change that takes place in us. But how does this accomplish our salvation?

Now this is one of those places where, according to human thought, we would still have this lovely intricate transaction which says, 'first this happens, then that happens'. It's almost a let-down to discover that the process of salvation is so simple that it's staring us in the face all the time. There's no mysticism about it. It is simply this: God chooses to forgive us.

That's how we're justified. God says, "You have sinned and I'm going to take your sins away."

The core process of salvation is forgiveness. We have sins that separate us from God and God is willing to take them away.

Glory of God

But this isn't a sufficient explanation. Why not? Because God doesn't forgive everyone.

If salvation was merely about God forgiving, then maybe he could just save everybody. So there must be something more. And indeed there is.

In Exodus 34, Moses asks to see the glory of God, and God agrees. When God's glory is revealed it is not how we might expect it. Moses doesn't get to see a really bright light, or an immensely loud noise, or any other spectacle we might imagine. Instead, the glory of God is contained in a declaration about his character. While we may be familiar with the words, we may not have noticed something odd about them.

> *Then the LORD came down in the cloud and stood there with him and proclaimed his name, the LORD. And he passed in front of Moses, proclaiming, "The LORD, the LORD, the compassionate and gracious God, slow to anger, abounding in love and faithfulness, maintaining love to thousands, and forgiving wickedness, rebellion and sin. Yet he does not leave the guilty unpunished; he punishes the children and their children for the sin of the fathers to the third and fourth generation. (Ex 34:5-7)*

Have you noticed that there's a paradox in the statement of the glory of God?

Here's what I mean. Apparently, the glory of God is both to forgive *and* to punish. It is both of them! It's not that God always forgives and it's not that God always punishes. He says that he forgives the wicked, but at the same time he doesn't leave the guilty unpunished. So which is it? Forgiveness or punishment?

The resolution to the paradox is that the glory of God is not in either the forgiveness or the punishment per se. Rather, the glory of God is in *balancing* between them. It is *the choice* between forgiveness and punishment that is the expression of God's glory.

You want to see the wonder of our Creator? Then meditate on his choice sometimes to forgive, and sometimes to condemn.

This is hard to do, so let's explore some more.

Constraint triangles

Why does God punish? Why is there even going to be a judgment? Why doesn't God say, "You know what? I'm just going to let everybody into the kingdom!" After all, God is God; he could, surely, do that. He could do anything, couldn't he?

This line of thinking could lead us astray. There are things that God cannot do. He cannot contradict himself, for example. That's why God cannot sin, nor even be tempted by sin.

In business there is a concept that can be expressed with a 'constraint triangle'. It reflects the idea that it is just not possible to have everything at the same time. To see a constraint triangle in action, imagine a triangle with each vertex (the pointy bits) labeled with Cost, Quality, and Time. The rule of the game is that you get to pick any two of the constraints, but cannot ever choose all three at the same time.

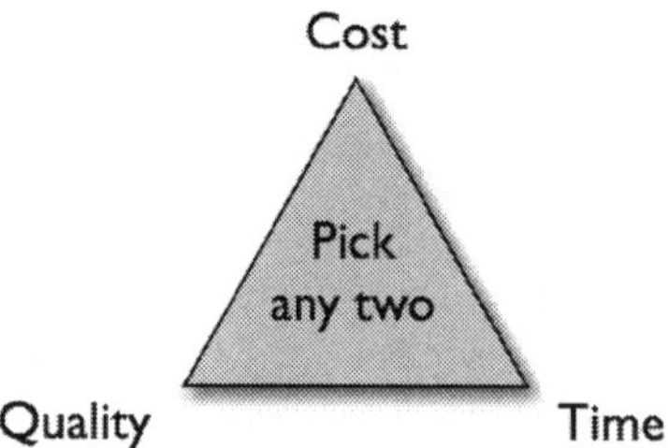

Suppose your client comes to you and says, "I'd like you to make me one of your widgets and I want you to give me the lowest price possible but the highest quality." So you say, "Ah! Then that's going to take me some time, as the only way I can cut the cost that much would be to slot it in the odd bits of time between other jobs." They get low cost, high quality, but at the expense of having to wait for it.

If they then say, "Oh no! I need that widget by tomorrow!" you might well respond, "Well, if you need it tomorrow, I'm going to have to charge you more because I'll have to pull people off other jobs to get your job done. It's a rush job and will cost you more. The alternative is to compromise on quality — it won't be the best work I can possibly do."

The constraint triangle expresses these fundamental tradeoffs. You can't have all three points in the 'constraints triangle' at the same time. They are in tension with each other; each one pulls away from the other two.

God's constraints

It appears that God is also under constraints. I think God would dearly love to have all of these things:

1. Human freewill (that we have real choices about who we are, and how we live);
2. Loving community (people together, fellowshipping, supporting and nourishing each other); and
3. Universal life (that everyone should get to be alive regardless of the choices they make).

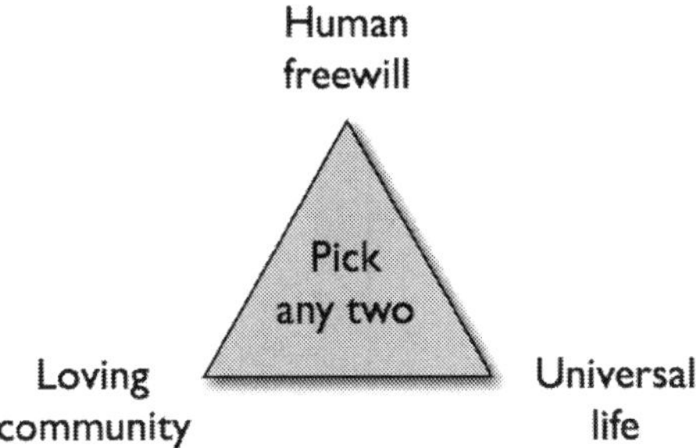

God would like all three, but not even God can have all three, because the three concepts together are mutually contradictory. Let's see why by considering a few examples.

Robots?

First, if God wants everybody to live, and also wants it to be a loving community, he would have to give up on human freewill.

Human freewill manifests itself in many ways. Sometimes, with God's help, it manifests itself by love and concern for others, but all too often, it manifests itself in selfishness and harm of others. If God wanted to have every human being form part of a loving community, regardless of their personal desires, he would have to remove their free will, to take away their freedom to choose their own way, their capacity for choice. They could not be permitted to harm or destroy. He would be able to satisfy the ideals of loving community and universal life, but at the cost of human freewill.

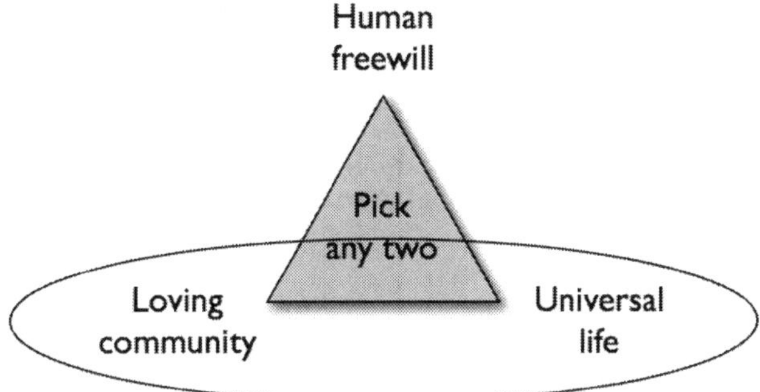

This is not acceptable to God. One of the fundamental things he has done right from the beginning is to provide individuals with the opportunity to choose. God didn't create mechanistic robots with preprogrammed responses. Instead he wanted individuals with individual sentience, and individual desires, who would perhaps choose partnership with him.

Removal of human freewill is not acceptable to God. So if he isn't prepared to give up on human freewill, what about the other two possibilities?

The World Today

One of the other options open to God (at least temporarily) is to give up on the loving community. This is really painful for God. But that is what he has done in the world today.

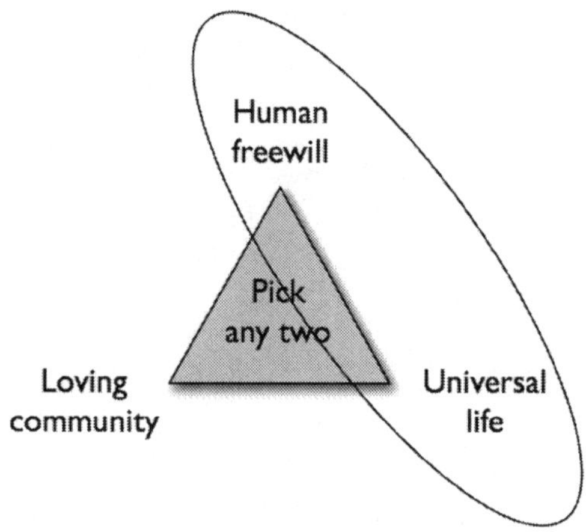

Today he says, "I am going to give people freewill, the ability to choose, and to allow their actions to have an impact on other people. I am going to let the sinner live. I'm going to allow the evil to work their evil. I'm not going to bring judgment — yet!"

Now there are times and places where even today God says, "This can go no further. I'm going to bring an end to this!" But by and large, the situation we are in today is that human freewill is exercised freely, and God allows all men and women to live.

The result is: today's society. We do not have a loving community in the world today.

Judgment

However, a time is coming, says God through Malachi, when we will see a clear distinction made between the righteous and the wicked:

> *"They will be mine," says the LORD Almighty, "in the day when I make up my treasured possession. I will spare them, just as in compassion a man spares his son who serves him. And you will again see the distinction between the righteous and the wicked, between those who serve God and those who do not. (Mal 3:17-18)*

In this future, God will ultimately relinquish the practice of allowing all to live. Instead, he will craft his loving community out of people who have freely chosen that that is what they want. His kingdom will be made up of people who out of their own free will wish to live and participate in loving community.

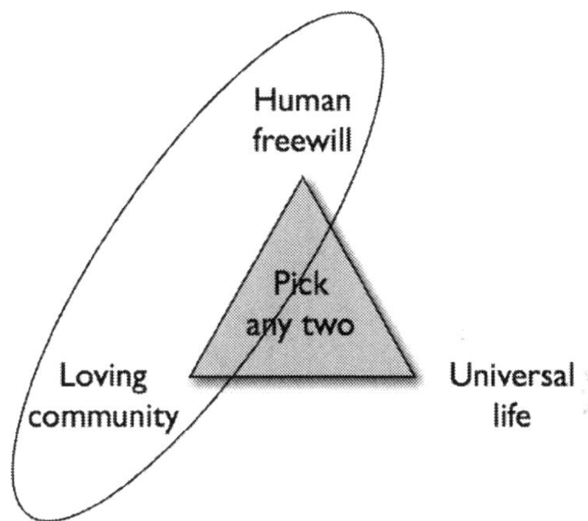

Automatically, this means that there are some who won't fit in that picture. Judgment, and hence punishment — the distinction between the righteous and the wicked — is simply a logical consequence of the ideals of both human freewill and a loving community.

The very fact that we have human freewill means that there are some people who choose that they do not want a loving community. They wouldn't want to live in one; they wouldn't want to participate in one.

So, at the end of the day, God has to say to those, "You will sleep forever, you will be oblivious, and cease to exist." God treats human freewill as so important that he's willing to respect people's decisions that they prefer eternal oblivion rather than eternal life in his kingdom. Their actual choice — in the extreme case, perhaps a Valhalla of self-indulgent greed — is not available, because one person's indulgence may be another person's pain or loss. This is not the loving community God intends to establish.

Seen this way, God's "punishment" is the outworking of the causal consequences of sin. Our sinful actions and thoughts are destructive of the health and wholeness that God longs for in us. Those damaged relationships, hardened hearts..., they all have a destructive effect on us.

Personal Examination

Even though we have discussed these three alternatives as God's choice and judgment as something God does, I think judgment is actually about the fulfillment of *our* choices.

I don't think of God as a legal judge, who says, "You have disobeyed the Law and hence must be punished." This again makes it sounds as if God is bound by some legal system.

Rather, I think of judgment as illumination, in which the truth is revealed. When the truth is revealed (like the sheep and goats) it becomes clear that some people do want wholeness and community and some do not. Seen in this light, the current framework of "freewill and universal life" is a compromise situation in which we get to work out who we are before the light is turned on.

The question for each of us is, What do I want? Deep down, in my inner being, do I really want righteousness? Do I want wholeness and community? Or do I actually prefer sin?

> *The LORD detests all the proud of heart. Be sure of this: They will not go unpunished. Through love and faithfulness sin is atoned for; through the fear of the LORD a man avoids evil. (Prov 16:5-6)*

On the day of judgment our hearts will be laid open, and on the basis of our deepest desire, the decision will be declared.

Summary

The paradox of the Glory of God: to balance the choice of when to forgive and when to condemn. God wants to build a society of beings who love one another through their free will, and he uses that choice as the basis of his judgment.

Discussion

1. How do you understand Exodus 34:5-7? What about the part about the 3rd and 4th generation? Suggest what may be meant by this.
2. Can you square the omnipotence of God with the idea that he is under constraints?
3. Most people are a bundle of mixed motives, and *judgment* seems to crystallize the situation too sharply. No one will stand revealed by the light as purely one thing or the other. How will God judge?
4. Is it possible that there are people who truly deep down would not want to participate in a loving society? What about you? What do you want, deep down? How do you know? How would God know that this is your desire?

Righteousness and sin

The Bible talks a lot about righteousness. What is it? How can we discern the difference between righteousness and unrighteousness?

Jesus is asked to give his opinion on a question like this.

> *One of them, an expert in the law, tested him with this question: "Teacher, which is the greatest commandment in the Law?" Jesus replied: "'Love the Lord your God with all your heart and with all your soul and with all your mind.' This is the first and greatest commandment. (Matt 22:35-38)*

But Jesus doesn't stop! That's not enough! He continues,

> *The second is like it, love your neighbor as yourself!*

I think Jesus is saying that the only way you can truly love God is by loving your neighbor.

Suppose you think you love God, that you have in your heart such warmth and love for God, yet you don't really care about anyone around you. If you have no sense of warmth or compassion for people, then the apostle John says you are a liar!

> *We love because he first loved us. If anyone says, "I love God," yet hates his brother, he is a liar. For anyone who does not love his brother, whom he has seen, cannot love God, whom he has not seen. And he has given us this command: Whoever loves God must also love his brother. (1 John 4:19-21)*

There's a real sense in which our love for God is manifest in our love for one another.

Maybe that's what Jesus meant when he said, "The second is just like it!" He's perhaps saying, "It's essentially the same thing. The first commandment is, You shall love God, and the second is the same, Love your neighbor." We should not think that these are two separate commandments, but two aspects of the same command.

If I want to know, "Am I loving God?" a very good test is to ask, "Am I loving my neighbor?"

What is sin?

Now let's look at righteousness from the opposite perspective.

What is sin?

Have you ever really asked yourself that question? If not, pause for a moment and think how you would define it. Suggest a couple of possible definitions? What is sin?

Here's one possible definition. We might say that sin is breaking the laws God has given, say, the ten commandments; i.e. if you break the ten commandments, that's sin.

Well, it certainly makes some sense: God gave commands and he expects people to follow them. On the other hand it doesn't seem a completely satisfactory definition. For example, most of us don't keep the Sabbath in the way laid out in the Law of Moses, so there's at least one of the ten commandments that we break. Yet the New Testament makes it clear that we are not sinning even though we do not follow that commandment, because the obligations of the complete Law are not laid on the Gentiles. For example:

> *One man considers one day more sacred than another; another man considers every day alike. Each one should be fully convinced in his own mind. He who regards one day as special, does so to the Lord. He who eats meat, eats to the Lord, for he gives thanks to God; and he who abstains, does so to the Lord and gives thanks to God. (Rom 14:5-6)*

Perhaps this only applies to ritual law. The ritual of the Law of Moses is no longer commanded, but the moral law of God still applies. This seems very reasonable, yet it still begs the classic question: is an act a sin because God prohibits it, or does God prohibit it because it is a sin?

Motivated by faith and love

Paul, in his letter to Rome (Rom 14:23), says that anything which is not from faith is sin. I find that quite useful. If my faith is motivating me to do something, and I choose to do something else, it's going to be sin. James gives a similar idea:

> *Anyone, then, who knows the good he ought to do and doesn't do it, sins. (Jas 4:17)*

Let's expand on this a bit. My *faith* expresses my best understanding of my relationship with God, and hence my relationship with other human beings too. If I choose to do something that is contrary to my understanding of what's important in building these relationships, then I am expressing a desire against love. And that will be sin. Similarly, if I avoid doing something when I know it is important to do it, then again I am not acting in love.

In contrast, everything Jesus did was motivated by his faith and love. His Father was in him and he was in his Father. He expressed righteousness as, "Not my will, but your will be done."

In this way, righteousness is about being willing to subject our freewill to God. He has given us freewill, the ability to choose. We get to use this in any way we wish. The highest path, the one that leads to eternal harmony, is to trust him, and show our love by actively loving others. Sin is the opposite of this. The attitude of sin says to God, "I know you want me to do this, but I actually want to do that other thing."

The path of faith and love is for us to take our natural will, and to give it back to God: "Not my will, but your will be done."

Sacrifice our wills

The most precious sacrifice we can give is our freewill. David wrote a Psalm about this, talking about himself as an echo of Jesus.

> *Sacrifice and offering you did not desire, but my ears you have pierced; burnt offerings and sin offerings you did not require. Then I said, "Here I am, I have come – it is written about me in the scroll. I desire to do your will, O my God; your law is within my heart." (Ps 40:6-8)*

It says that God did not desire sacrifice and offering. Actually, God *did* want them to bring burnt offerings and sin offerings; the Law was very clear. The Law said, "You are required to bring a lamb, cut its throat and pour out its blood."

Yet here, inspired by the same Eternal Spirit that provided the Law, David says in effect, "It's not the dead animal that you care about, is it, God? It's not the blood being spilled that you want. What you, God, care about is what is going on in my heart when I perform the sacrifice, not the sacrifice itself."

It's Gethsemane! I desire to do your will, O Lord, not mine. A daily Gethsemane for each one of us. Not my will, but yours be done. I walk humbly with you, my God. (Mic 6:8)

Humbly means that I don't assert, 'I do what *I* want to do.' *Humbly* means that I don't challenge the judgment of God when he calls something sin. *Humbly* means I don't argue with him that something can't possibly be sin simply because I — my flesh — wants it so much. No! Instead, *humbly* means that I say to him, "I will learn from you. I will take my standards from you. I come to do your will, not my own desire."

Accepting God's standard

Look at Psalm 51:3-4, quoted in the New Testament in connection with salvation (in Rom 3:4).

> *For I know my transgressions, and my sin is always before me. Against you, you only, have I sinned and done what is evil in your sight, so that you are proved right when you speak and justified when you judge. (Ps 51:3-4)*

David wrote this Psalm after he finally realized the enormity of what he had done. It started with lust for Bathsheba and ended with the murder of Uriah, working its way, step by step, through deceit and self-justification.

Now he has awoken to his sin. Now he pours himself out before God.

> *Have mercy on me, O God, according to your unfailing love; according to your great compassion blot out my transgressions. Wash away all my iniquity and cleanse me from my sin. (Ps 51:1-2)*

And then he introduces a strange phrase in that fourth verse: *"...so that you are proved right when you speak and justified when you judge."*

What's going on? What does it mean?

I think David is saying: "I'm going to stand up and I'm going to say: I sinned!" I think he is making an open, clear declaration of his sin, so that it may be known that God is right when he said that David had sinned. God is proved right; he is justified in his judgment of David because David is supporting God's declaration.

Admit to sin

When we have our sins, the ones which we like to hold on to, we can fall into the trap of self-justification. We might start saying to ourselves, 'They're not really sins..."

If we start saying that, then we are doing exactly the opposite of what David did. We are not justifying God. Rather, we are making God out to be a liar.

If God says that to do this or that is destructive, if he says that this action damages you, or other people — or it damages your relationship with him! — and we say, "No! It doesn't!" then we are calling God a liar.

The first step to sacrificing our will is to admit our sin.

Some sins are almost fashionable, like being impatient or stubborn, or not tolerating fools easily, whereas others are not — being unkind or uncaring, lacking empathy, being jealous or hateful towards others. I think we find it is easier to admit to fashionable sins than the ones we consider more ugly. Yet both kinds can be destructive.

Look at the cartoon of the man in a card shop trying to buy a card. He has a worried expression, and asks the assistant, "Do you have a card that stops short of saying 'I'm sorry' yet vaguely hints at some wrongdoing?"

That's what we are like, all too often! In our church services we sometimes pray, "Lord, we recognize that we're sinners before you; forgive our sin." We admit that we are sinners, but only in very general terms. If someone came up to one of us and said, "You're a sinner because you did this... and this... etc." we would probably be highly offended! Who does our accuser think he or she is to be so bold!

So we don't mind vaguely hinting at some wrongdoing...

" Do you have a card that stops short of saying *' I'm sorry '* yet vaguely hints at some wrongdoing ? "

We have to be honest with ourselves, and honest with God. We must be frank about what is sin in our lives, so that God is proved right when he judges. He wants us to sacrifice ourselves over to him.

> *Therefore, I urge you, brothers, in view of God's mercy, to offer your bodies as living sacrifices, holy and pleasing to God (Rom 12:1)*

God wants us to admit that our lives belong to him, that our wills belong to him.

If we can genuinely admit that our sin is sin, then he will take it away from us. But that requires is to be truly honest with God — and indeed with ourselves!

I came across wonderfully enigmatic saying that captures this:

> *Forgiveness is giving up all hope of a better past.*

Just mull over that for a while.

Summary

The essence of sin is destructiveness, while the essence of righteousness is to love others truly. God wants us to admit that we are sinners, so that he may work in our lives to have us overcome our natural inclinations.

Discussion

1. Have you ever confessed your sin to another human being? How did it make you feel?
2. When do you find it hard to submit your will to God?
3. Are there any ways in which we can love God that have no impact on others?

The salvation process

Let's pull together the threads we've been exploring, and address a fundamental question.

How are we saved?

I think the Bible consistently presents salvation as a process that God engages in with us. Here I've broken it up into five separate steps. I suspect that it could be broken up differently, but these five will do us for now.

1. God declares our sin and his love;
2. We agree, and want to be different;
3. He forgives, and liberates us from our guilt;
4. We trust, and participate in his work of transforming us;
5. He completes the work in resurrection and judgment.

When God declares our sin, we have to agree with his declaration if we want salvation to go anywhere. That's an essential step. If we say, "I know you think I'm a sinner, God, but I think I'm okay," then salvation stops at that point. It's like an alcoholic who doesn't admit to being an alcoholic. The process of healing doesn't even begin; there's a huge internal barrier that needs to be overcome.

That's not to say that God gives up at this point. Rather he keeps working and working encouraging us to look inside ourselves and see what he sees.

It is critical that we come to a point where we agree with him, and come to desire something different from what we are and what we do. "I don't like being angry, I don't like lusting, I don't like coveting — at least, I wish I didn't like being angry, or lusting, or coveting..."

So, we desire to be different. We desire to be free from the rulership of sin. Then — and this is the liberating step of salvation — he forgives us.

He *forgives us*!

It's as simple as that. He says: "If you want to be different, if you want to be righteous, I'll treat you *as though you are righteous*. All these things you've done in the past, let's just move them aside, get rid of them! Imagine you're starting anew today; none of the past is dragging you down; nothing you've done in the past is holding you back. Now stand up! You're cleansed! Now, who will go for us?" He's hoping for the response, "Here am I! Send me!" (Is 6:8)

He stands us upright. He liberates us from our guilt, and we trust in him.

Trust is the essence of faith here. We trust in two aspects; we trust that God is truly liberating us, and we trust in the path he has laid out for us. Thus we are energized and empowered to participate in his work of making us new.

> *For we are God's workmanship, created in Christ Jesus to do good works, which God prepared in advance for us to do. (Eph 2:10)*

Notice that we don't do the work by ourselves. It is God's work. He is doing it, but he also expects us to join in.

Some Christians suggest that any idea of us participating in God's work of saving us is like saying that we are saving ourselves, or that we are being saved by works. I don't think this follows at all. Scripture is very clear that we need to participate in God's work of saving us. It is faith working itself out in practice.

Here's an analogy: We're stuck in a pit, we've fallen down and simply can't get out, maybe we can hardly move. God is there rescuing us; he reaches down and offers to free us if we wish it. We manifest our desire to be rescued by reaching out to him and hanging on to him. We're not saving ourselves, but that doesn't mean that we just sit around and do nothing.

Finally, the capstone of the salvation process comes in the resurrection and judgment. At that point, the deepest desires of our hearts will be fully carried out, the war within ourselves will be over. God's creative work will be completed.

1. God declares our sin and his love

Let's look at these steps in a little more detail. We'll begin in Hebrews.

> *In the past God spoke to our forefathers through the prophets at many times and in various ways, but in these last days he has spoken to us by his Son. (Heb 1:1-2)*

When Jesus was sent, God was speaking through him. I don't think it just means his words. Everything Jesus did or said, even his very being, was part of God speaking to us, telling us fundamental truths about himself, and about us, and about our salvation.

I think the first few verses of John's gospel are saying the same thing. In the beginning God spoke his word — let there be light, let the sea bring forth living creatures, and so on. Everything God ever did was done through his word, through the things he said. And now, everything God has been saying is embodied in this human being, Jesus Christ. Here's how Jesus himself describes it, speaking about the spiritually dead:

> *I tell you the truth, a time is coming and has now come when the dead will hear the voice of the Son of God and those who hear will live. (John 5:25)*

Thus, when God declares our sin, or when God declares his love for us, it's no surprise that these declarations come through loud and clear in everything Jesus has been saying and doing. We can look at the work of Jesus and see God both declaring our sin, and declaring his love for us. "It's not my word," says Jesus, "they are the words of my Father who sent me." (John 14:24)

So whether through Jesus or elsewhere, when God says: "You sin," it's not for us to say, "No I don't!"

Even Job has to hear the same message, even though the narrator describes him as blameless (Job 1:1). Yet in the course of the bitter and wearisome discourse, he comes to the point of claiming to have done nothing wrong before God. He comes close to saying: "God, you have wronged me!" God challenges him in his second speech.

> *Would you discredit my justice? Would you condemn me to justify yourself? (Job 40:8)*

We sometimes fall into the same trap. We sometimes say, "God isn't treating me right! God isn't treating me the way I think I should be treated; I am better than this! I am more important than this!" — and now we are discrediting God's justice in order to justify ourselves.

When Job saw how close he had come to making this kind of declaration before God, his response was one of horror. He realized that within himself is the power of behemoth, the force of sin. It is so powerful, even within an incredible man like Job.

2. We agree, and want to be different

Finally we listen to God. Like Job, we acknowledge how powerful the flesh is, and how weak we are in the face of it.

Paul describes it this way:

> *We know that the law is spiritual; but I am unspiritual, sold as a slave to sin. I do not understand what I do. For what I want to do I do not do, but what I hate I do. (Rom 7:14-15)*

I know what I want to be like. Even though I find it hard, perhaps impossible sometimes, I still know that I aspire to be righteous, to live my life in total service to my God. Whether or not I succeed on a day-to-day basis is not the point; the real point is what I aspire to. In my deepest heart, do I truly want to be righteous or not?

Christ is there as the supreme example that we aspire to. He is the model for our lives, and by his very being, is an encouragement to us.

This is how Paul describes it.

> *My dear children, for whom I am again in the pains of childbirth until Christ is formed in you. (Gal 4:19)*

That idea — Christ formed within me — captures wonderfully what we aspire to. That's what I want, sometimes even in the moment when I am caught up in sin.

3. He forgives, and liberates us from our guilt

If we want to be righteous, then God has a wonderful way to help us. He forgives us! He simply does not count our sin against us.

Strangely enough, this is a really hard concept for us to grasp, despite it being so simple.

For some reason, it seems to be very hard for us to really feel that we have been forgiven by God. So at the risk of overdoing things, let's describe it again, from differing angles. This is how Paul describes it:

> *Justified through faith, we have peace with God. (Rom 5:1)*

Think about that! That's the situation disciples of Christ are in today! We have gone through the first couple of steps; we've listened to God; we've understood and we do want to be different, no longer serving sin but serving God. So now the next step is that he forgives. And we are at peace with God! We are not at enmity with him. God is not angry at us. He is not holding us blameworthy. Rather we are at peace with him.

Indeed, we are in a covenant of forgiveness, whereby God does not hold our sins against us, as Paul says.

> *God was reconciling the world to himself in Christ, not counting men's sins against them. (2 Cor 5:19)*

We still sin, but we regret our sins and present them to God, and he says, "Don't be afraid, I am not counting your sins against you." And that's another sin that is simply moved away. We are sinless in God's eyes! That's what it means to have peace with God. It's a tremendous situation that we're in!

Do you believe that? Do I?

"Lord I believe. Help my unbelief."

God wants us to believe in his forgiveness, so that we will not be afraid of him. He wants us to come near to him, to allow him to develop a close and loving relationship with us.

> *Let us draw near to God with a sincere heart in full assurance of faith, having our hearts sprinkled to cleanse us from a guilty conscience and having our bodies washed with pure water. (Heb 10:22)*

The writer notes many key factors about drawing near to God; faith; our hearts sprinkled; cleansed from a guilty conscience; and bodies washed in water. Many of these are standard in Christian discussion. But have you thought about being cleansed from a guilty conscience?

A guilty conscience means we haven't adopted God's forgiveness properly. If I'm feeling guilty about things that I've done, that means I don't believe that God has taken my sin away. Put another way, this passage encourages and exhorts us to come to God with the confidence that we don't have to feel guilty. Why not? Because God has forgiven. Everything!

Those things we are ashamed of, those things that we have difficulty admitting even to ourselves, let alone to other people, God has forgiven!

The way God takes them away is for us to talk to him about them. If we just hide them in our heart, pretending that they don't exist, we're not being honest with ourselves; we're not being honest with God. We're still making God out to be a liar.

But if we just have the courage — and it does take courage — to say, "I know this is a sin, I'm really sorry. I wish I wasn't so attracted to that particular kind of behavior. Please forgive me," then he says, "I'll take the guilt of it away."

Not that we won't struggle with that sort of behavior. The more that we sin, the more our minds and flesh demand more of it. When we give in to sin we make it harder for ourselves. Even so, God does take away the guilt. He takes away the blame, so that we no longer need be dragged down by our sin.

Like Isaiah we can be freed from our sense of failure, so that we stand up and declare, "Here am I, send me!"

4. We trust, and participate in his work of transforming us

Let's go back to Paul in Romans.

> *Therefore, since we have been justified through faith, we have peace with God through our Lord Jesus Christ, through whom we have gained access by faith into this grace in which we now stand. (Rom 5:1-2)*

I don't think the previous lack of access to 'this grace' was due to God keeping us out, but that we didn't want to have access, we didn't want to be different. Or maybe that we were too afraid, or too bound up in our earthly woes, to want to have access.

The role of Jesus is to bring us out of hiding to meet God, to draw us, to encourage us.

Through Christ, I now have access to God. I want to be in God's presence whereas, before Christ, I might not have wanted that. It might have been harder for me to see that God's way is the way I truly want.

> *Not only so, but we also rejoice in our sufferings, because we know that suffering produces perseverance; perseverance, character; and character, hope. And hope does not disappoint us, because God has poured out his love into our hearts by the Holy Spirit, whom he has given us. (Rom 5:3-4)*

We have a spirit within us which resonates with Christ, which emphasizes the hope we have, and gives meaning to the struggle we have. We trust in God and participate in his transforming work, making us different on the inside. It's like a 'microwave' which heats the chicken from the inside out. His work of changing us from wrongness to rightness is from the inside out.

The incident in Ezekiel shows how God accomplishes things with our participation. God says to Ezekiel, "Stand!" And Ezekiel said, "He stood me up" (Ezek 2:1-2). Note that God didn't say, "Stand! And get up on your own two feet!" Rather he said to stand, and then empowered the prophet by picking him up.

It's the same with us. He calls us to follow him, to give our lives to God, to walk away from the destructiveness of sin, and then he gives us the strength and ability to accomplish this.

I used to overlook this aspect of God's involvement when reading Philippians:

> *Therefore, my dear friends, as you have always obeyed — not only in my presence, but now much more in my absence — continue to work out your salvation with fear and trembling,*

If we stop there, it leaves us with the impression that we've got a whole lot of work to do, that it's going to be a tedious slog, and we'd better just get on our feet and make it work.

But that's not what Paul is saying. Just follow the whole sentence into the next verse.

> *Therefore, my dear friends, as you have always obeyed — not only in my presence, but now much more in my absence — continue to work out your salvation with fear and trembling, for it is God who works in you to will and to act according to his good purpose. (Phil 2:12-13)*

Look at that. It is *God* who works in us!

The working out of our salvation is not one of earning our salvation, but is more like working throughout the period of our salvation. God has rescued us. He saved us when we decided to move from death to life at our baptisms. Moreover, God *will* save us when Christ declares us righteous at the judgment. And finally, God is in the process of saving us now. Now is the time of our salvation! Now is when we are being transformed. It's God's work; we participate in it, we throw ourselves into it wholeheartedly. It is not going to be easy but, fundamentally, it is God's work.

Look again at that phrase in Philippians:

> *It is God who works in you, to will and to act according to his good purpose.*

So God not only gives us the strength to do the things that he calls us to do, he also helps us to *want* the things that he wants. That's what "to will" means. He helps me with the struggle I have when I say, "I wish I didn't want this so badly, and I wish I did want that." God works at that level as well, helping me to want the right things; the things I want to want.

5. He completes the work in resurrection and judgment

We'll have a lot more to say about the resurrection and judgment in later sections, so we'll be brief here.

> *And so we know and rely on the love God has for us. God is love. Whoever lives in love lives in God, and God in him. In this way, love is made complete among us so that we will have confidence on the day of judgment, because in this world we are like him. There is no fear in love. But perfect love drives out fear, because fear has to do with punishment. The one who fears is not made perfect in love. (1 John 4:16-18)*

If we let him work on us to transform us, to have Christ *formed within us* so that we are *like him*, then indeed we can have confidence in the day of judgment.

Not because we deserve life; we haven't earned it at all.

Rather because God has forgiven our sin, has taken it away, and is not counting our sin against us. He will fulfill the desire that he has grown within us — with our willingness and participation.

Summary

Salvation starts with God declaring both our sin and his love. When we agree and want to be different, he freely forgives us and liberates us from our guilt. We trust in him and participate in his work of transforming us, which he completes in resurrection and judgment.

Discussion

1. Discuss each of the steps in the salvation process in turn. Do they each make sense? Are there any other steps you would want to add in the description of the process?
2. What role does Jesus fulfill in each of the steps of the salvation process?
3. Is it okay to sin now that we've been forgiven? Go beyond a simple yes/no answer.

Savior

You may recall that, many sections ago, I claimed that the Bible gives us two fundamental reasons for Jesus' death.

1. His death is supposed to have a profound and transforming effect on us. It is the beginning of a process in which we must thoroughly participate. And,
2. His personal sacrifice played a major role in the development and perfecting of Christ himself.

We have explored the first in quite a bit of detail. Here's a quick summary of what we have discussed:

- The fundamental purpose of the sacrifice of Christ is to draw people to God. God did not need Jesus to die. Rather he allowed him to be murdered as a clarion call to us all.
- When Jesus gave his life, he gave the whole of his life; every aspect — he gave his 'living' to us — so that we could live.
- We must be changed. We should not try to make excuses for our sins or blame someone else, but must accept our need to be different.
- Salvation is through faith and forgiveness. God wants his people to come to him in faith, and he reaches out in forgiveness. Forgiveness is meaningless without our response.

Now it is time to turn our attention to the second above: the claim that Jesus' personal sacrifice played a major role in the development and perfecting of Jesus himself. This is a dramatic — even shocking — idea, but one that the Bible refers to on numerous occasions.

To understand this dimension of his death, we shall first step back and examine Jesus' role in our salvation. We will look at the role of savior from a number of different perspectives to gain a broad understanding of who Jesus is and why God appointed him. This will deepen our understanding of our own salvation, as well as providing context in which we can understand Jesus' own need for spiritual development. Then we shall be able to appreciate Golgotha as a critical step in that development.

God is our Savior

Jesus is our savior. Right?

Well, yes. But let's first get one fundamental fact straight, one that the Bible is very clear about: *God* is the savior. Just listen to Isaiah:

> *I, even I, am the LORD, and apart from me there is no Savior. (Is 43:11)*

The context makes it clear that this is a claim of God himself. He is countering the empty claims about the idols of the day, who cannot help anyone. He is savior. "Apart from me," says God, "No one can save."

In the NIV, there are 31 occasions in the Old Testament where the word *savior* is used; all of them apply to God. This isn't just an Old Testament phenomenon. Even in the New Testament, of the 24 references to *savior* eight of them (one-third) refer explicitly to God as our savior. For example:

> *Paul, an apostle of Christ Jesus by the command of God our Savior and of Christ Jesus our hope… (1 Tim 1:1)*

The others apply to Jesus, unsurprisingly. For example,

> *Grace and peace from God the Father and Christ Jesus our Savior. (Titus 1:4)*

This raises a question: how can Jesus be savior when Isaiah has just told us that there is no savior apart from God? Happily, Isaiah himself provides the key:

> *[God] saw that there was no one, he was appalled that there was no one to intervene; so his own arm worked salvation for him, and his own righteousness sustained him. (Is 59:16)*

As we will see later, Jesus is God's "arm" and manifesting God himself. He is the agent of God's work, the mechanism by which God is saving us. Jesus is not a savior *apart from* God. Rather, God is savior, and by extension, so is Jesus. His name even expresses this: *Jesus* in Greek is *Yeh sous*, which means *God saves.*

An intermediary from God

All of this begs a question: why doesn't God just act as savior directly? Why does he appoint Jesus in that role?

I've heard all sorts of answers to this. For example, I have heard people suggest that God cannot sympathize properly with our situation; that because God is sinless and omnipotent he would not be able to properly appreciate how hard our struggle is. This idea seems to be drawn from the following verse in Hebrews:

> *For we do not have a high priest who is unable to sympathize with our weaknesses, but we have one who has been tempted in every way, just as we are — yet was without sin. (Heb 4:15)*

On the face of it, that may be a reasonable inference to draw from this verse. But I don't think the inference is valid. In fact, it seems quite problematic because it has the effect of diminishing God. It is just another way of placing the need for Christ on God, rather than on us, suggesting that Christ made up for one of God's supposed limitations.

As we've seen before, it is much more reasonable to begin with the assumption that any limitations are ours rather than God's. When we do this, we see another possible interpretation of the verse: that even though God can indeed sympathize one hundred percent with our state, it's just that *we find it hard to believe that he does.*

In this context God says, "I know you find it hard to believe that I can truly sympathize with your struggle and temptation. Well, let me reassure you by appointing someone just like you to be at my right hand."

So he appoints Jesus, and *we gain confidence* that someone in heaven is truly able to sympathize with our weakness. In this interpretation, God is again working to help us with our lack of faith in him, our inability to come to him in perfect trust.

We can go further. Here's what Moses told the Israelites:

> *The LORD your God will raise up for you a prophet like me from among your own brothers. You must listen to him. For this is what you asked of the LORD your God at Horeb [Sinai] on the day of the assembly when you said, 'Let us not hear the voice of the LORD our God nor see this great fire anymore, or we will die.'" (Deut 18:15-16)*

Having shaky trust in God's compassion and sympathy is only part of the problem. We are terrified by the Almighty!

A whole nation of people — people just like us — were filled with dread in the presence of God. We come to the foot of a mount like Sinai and see the power of heaven ready to be unleashed, and we are terrified! We quake with fear!

Finally, we admit we are scared and acknowledge that we don't know how to come close to this awesome presence. "You go, Moses; see if God will talk through you and you bring his message to us," they said. Anything to put a little distance between us and the dread mightiness of heaven.

I wonder if God was sad, wishing that people could trust his words of love and assurance. But God is God. He knows who we are, and he pragmatically deals with the world as it is, not as he wishes it might be. He is the ultimate realist. The people needed an intermediary. They needed someone with whom they could directly relate, and God compassionately acceded to their need, and the Law was given through Moses.

In each case, God acts to give us confidence; he appoints an intermediary in our salvation. We are afraid, or we worry that God cannot sympathize, so he acts to reassure us.

Jesus the Prophet

Do we think we are any different from them? Even Daniel quaked and collapsed at the sight of an angel cloaked in the power of heaven (Dan 10:8-9). We are just the same. The same fear, the same desire to hide. So God continues to Moses:

> *'What they say is good. I will raise up for them a prophet like you from among their brothers; I will put my words in his mouth, and he will tell them everything I command him. If anyone does not listen to my words that the prophet speaks in my name, I myself will call him to account.' (Deut 18:17-19)*

God provides the ultimate prophet! Raised up among us, just like us. He will speak God's words and call the people to account. And he will bless us by turning us from our destructiveness and slavery to sin, and save us to serve the God of the universe.

Jesus, the Messiah of God, is that man Moses was prophesying about, as Peter declares in a speech in the temple in Jerusalem. The whole speech is worth reading, but here's how he ends it:

> *By faith in the name of Jesus, this man whom you see and know was made strong. It is Jesus' name and the faith that comes through him that has given this complete healing to him, as you can all see....*
>
> *For Moses said, 'The Lord your God will raise up for you a prophet like me from among your own people; you must listen to everything he tells you. Anyone who does not listen to him will be completely cut off from among his people.'*
>
> *Indeed, all the prophets from Samuel on, as many as have spoken, have foretold these days. And you are heirs of the prophets and of the covenant God made with your fathers. He said to Abraham, 'Through your offspring all peoples on earth will be blessed.' When God raised up his servant, he sent him first to you to bless you by turning each of you from your wicked ways." (Acts 3:16, 22-26)*

Jesus, like Moses, was faithful within God's household, though Jesus served as a son rather than simply a servant (Heb 3:1-6). But there was another critical similarity. Like Moses, Jesus was one of us, raised up from among our brothers, from among people like us. This is how it is put in Hebrews:

> *Since the children have flesh and blood, he too shared in their humanity (Heb 2:14)*

The Bible is very clear, emphatic even, that Jesus was fully human.

Jesus, the same flesh as ours, and just like one of us. As such, Jesus would not terrify the people. He spoke boldly as God's prophet, and the people listened gladly.

Though insistent for people to make the right ways of God the priority in their lives, his love and compassion (which reflect his Father) makes it easier to come close to him. God's plan worked out perfectly.

Summary

God is our savior, but because of fear people like us have always needed God to work through intermediaries, to appoint representatives to speak for him. So God has provided the ultimate prophet, Jesus; he is one of us, yet he speaks perfectly for God. He is our savior.

Discussion

1. Before reading this section, did you think of God as savior? If not, why not?
2. Discuss the interpretations suggested for Heb 4:15, and see which viewpoint you find most compelling.
3. What would it be like to be face to face with God? What examples can you think of in the Bible?

Prophet leaders

In the last section, we explored a couple of reasons for God working his plan of salvation through Jesus. As a prophet sent from God, Jesus is the culmination of a long and illustrious history. Here's how he describes it in a parable:

> *"A man planted a vineyard, rented it to some farmers and went away for a long time. At harvest time he sent a servant to the tenants so they would give him some of the fruit of the vineyard. But the tenants beat him and sent him away empty-handed. He sent another servant, but that one also they beat and treated shamefully and sent away empty-handed. He sent still a third, and they wounded him and threw him out.*
>
> *"Then the owner of the vineyard said, 'What shall I do? I will send my son, whom I love; perhaps they will respect him.'*
>
> *"But when the tenants saw him, they talked the matter over. 'This is the heir,' they said. 'Let's kill him, and the inheritance will be ours.' So they threw him out of the vineyard and killed him.*
>
> *"What then will the owner of the vineyard do to them? He will come and kill those tenants and give the vineyard to others."*
>
> *When the people heard this, they said, "May this never be!" (Luke 20:9-16)*

Throughout history God has always appealed to people through great men and women, prophets who were separated to the task of drawing others to God. Biblically, a prophet is someone who proclaims God's message to people. They may say something about the future, but they are equally likely to talk about the past. Either way, their real interest is the present, helping their listeners to connect with God. These mighty individuals bring God's message and reach out to the people around them. Here's a short list:

- Abraham was chosen by God so that he would "direct his children and his household after him to keep the way of the LORD by doing what is right and just" (Gen 18:19).
- Joseph was taken captive down to Egypt and used by God to save not only his own family but the whole ancient world.
- Moses was brought up a prince in Egypt, but ended up being a humble shepherd, and in that capacity he saved and led the nation of Israel, bringing them out of slavery to the border of the promised land.
- Deborah, Gideon, and Samuel, were each appointed by God in times of crisis to lead and judge the nation.
- David, a songwriter, prophet, and king, described as a man after God's own heart.
- Hezekiah, also a king, close to dying, poured out his heart to God on behalf of the people.
- Zerubbabel the governor, worked with prophets like Haggai and Zechariah to reestablish the nation after they returned from captivity in Babylon.
- Peter the apostle, reached out to the nation of Israel: "Men and brothers, this thing has been done in front of you," he says.
- Paul brought the message of salvation not only to the Jewish people but more widely, to bring Jew and Gentile together.

The list could go on and on. God has always been working through prophet leaders, because people best hear the word of God from someone like themselves.

Standing in the breach

For our sake, God looks for individuals who can truly speak his words, who authentically represent the things he is looking for, who can nurture others in the ways of God. So, what happens when God can't find someone? When his word of salvation is not getting through?

An example occurs in Ezekiel, which was written around the time of the destruction of the southern kingdom of Judah. According to Ezekiel a rottenness pervades the whole nation:

> *There is a conspiracy of her princes within her like a roaring lion tearing its prey; they devour people, take treasures and precious things and make many widows within her.*

> *Her priests do violence to my law and profane my holy things; they do not distinguish between the holy and the common; they teach that there is no difference between the unclean and the clean; and they shut their eyes to the keeping of my Sabbaths, so that I am profaned among them.*
>
> *Her officials within her are like wolves tearing their prey; they shed blood and kill people to make unjust gain.*
>
> *Her prophets whitewash these deeds for them by false visions and lying divinations. They say, 'This is what the Sovereign LORD says' – when the LORD has not spoken.*
>
> *The people of the land practice extortion and commit robbery; they oppress the poor and needy and mistreat the alien, denying them justice. (Ezek 22:25-29)*

It's a terrible situation! Prince, priest, official, prophet, and people all come under condemnation. Corruption from the top to the bottom! They are a nation desperately in need of correction, of healing. They are a nation on the verge of being destroyed because of their rejection of the principles of God. And God says:

> *I looked for a man among them who would build up the wall and stand before me in the gap on behalf of the land so I would not have to destroy it, but I found none (Ezek 22:30).*

The wall is broken down! The nation is defenseless against condemnation. Who will stand in the breach in the wall, and provide a reason to delay judgment? They are like a city without any protection, naked to any invading army. Who will lead this people? Who will guide this people? Who will change them?

Jeremiah's there!

But he's done all he can and they don't listen to him. In the end God has said, "I need you to stop praying, Jeremiah; it's not going to work any more." (Jer 7:16)

What a tragedy!

The arm of the Lord

What happens with Israel is a picture of the situation with the whole of humanity. Here's how Isaiah puts it:

> *Truth is nowhere to be found, and whoever shuns evil becomes a prey. The LORD looked and was displeased that there was no justice. He saw that there was no one, he was appalled that there was no one to intervene; so his own arm worked salvation for him, and his own righteousness sustained him (Is 59:15-16).*

God looks around. Where is the savior among the people? Where is the prophet who is going to arise and lead them?

This may have been written for Isaiah's time originally, but the message is timeless. Where is the prophet who is going to arise and lead us? Who will show us the path out of the valley of the shadow of death, and bring us into life that is truly life?

God looks at the sweep of history, and sees that there isn't going to be one. Without his personal intervention, there is never going to be a prophet who will be able to speak the words of God one hundred percent, a prophet who never has doubts about himself, who can speak for God without wavering or faltering, and who can bring his whole heart, mind, strength, and soul to the work of God.

Faced with this lack, God's own arm worked salvation for him. Who or what is this "arm"? It is Jesus. Listen to these words of Isaiah where he uses "arm" as a metaphor for Christ working salvation on behalf of God.

> *Who has believed our message and to whom has the arm of the LORD been revealed? He grew up before him like a tender shoot, and like a root out of dry ground. He had no beauty or majesty to attract us to him, nothing in his appearance that we should desire him. He was despised and rejected by men, a man of sorrows, and familiar with suffering. (Is 53:1-3)*

This whole passage was looking ahead to the sufferings of the Messiah. He is God's right arm. In effect, God says, "No one was just going to arise; I had to do it. I had to do it through a son, as an extension of myself."

And so the power of the eternal spirit overshadowed a young Jewish girl, and a son was conceived. A child, one of us, but who would grow up and show himself to be the son of God, in every sense possible.

Parable of the fig tree

Here's another parable Jesus used to describe his work:

> *A man had a fig tree, planted in his vineyard, and he went to look for fruit on it, but did not find any. So he said to the man who took care of the vineyard, 'For three years now I've been coming to look for fruit on this fig tree and haven't found any. Cut it down! Why should it use up the soil?'*
>
> *'Sir,' the man replied, 'leave it alone for one more year, and I'll dig around it and fertilize it. If it bears fruit next year, fine! If not, then cut it down.' (Luke 13:6-9)*

At first sight it looks like there is a disagreement between the owner and the vinedresser; as though the owner is saying, "Cut this thing down," and the vinedresser says, "No, no, no! Please don't..." as if he were pleading on behalf of the fig tree, trying to change the owner's mind.

I don't think that's what's going on at all. Here's another way to look at what's happening.

First of all the owner makes an assessment, "This fig tree is fruitless; it deserves to be cut down." The vinedresser has the same opinion. If you look at his response, he never disagrees with the owner's judgment, not even by insinuation. There's no disagreement there, no dispute. This tree needs to bear fruit, and if it does not, it should be cut down.

But that's not all. The vinedresser speaks up with an offer, "If you are willing, I will work with this tree for one more year. I offer for us to see if more of my personal time and effort will make a difference to this tree. If it still doesn't produce fruit, well, we'll have done everything we could possibly have tried. Then we'll cut it down."

You see the point? One has come amongst us, to work with us, to see if we can be nurtured and encouraged to bear fruit. God owns the vineyard; Jesus is the vinedresser. He offers to work to transform us, so that we bear fruit for God. He will stand in the breach, delaying and removing the need for condemnation.

Moses played that role with the Israelites in the wilderness:

> *[God] said he would destroy them – had not Moses, his chosen one, stood in the breach before him to keep his wrath from destroying them. (Ps 106:23)*

Moses was willing to take the burden of leading the people, and with his willingness, a new possibility opened up. With his engagement, faith and righteousness were again possible within this people.

Our prophet leader, our savior judge, is among us now. Jesus the Christ, who lived his life preaching first to the people of Israel, now has spread his message to the world. He's nurturing, fertilizing, watering…

Will we listen? Will we grow? Will we bear fruit?

Summary

Prophet leaders were appointed to rescue the people from their destructive ways and urge them to listen to what God was saying. Mighty though they were, these prophets were always less than perfect. God still had to intervene with his own voice, his own right arm, Jesus his son.

Discussion

1. Remind yourself of the prophet leaders introduced in this section. Can you think of any others?
2. Why does it make sense for God to use prophet leaders? Does he have a choice?

Humanity of Jesus

Jesus, our savior; one of us in order to give us confidence that one in heaven understands what it is like to be human. But what does it mean for him to be human?

Consider the following verse, talking about Jesus,

> *Since the children have flesh and blood, he too shared in their humanity... (Heb 2:14)*

The writer is trying to drive the point home that Jesus didn't merely *appear* to be human, but that he really was, that he *shared in our humanity!* The same verse feels even more emphatic in the King James version

> *Forasmuch then as the children are partakers of flesh and blood, he also himself likewise took part of the same... (KJV)*

Look at that string of emphasis words: *he also himself likewise...*

Even though he was God's *son*, he was one of us! This verse in Hebrews makes it clear that Jesus had the same nature as us. He shared in our human nature, the same flesh and blood, and faced the same kinds of temptations, forces and pressures that we do.

Not convinced? Look a few verses later:

> *For this reason he had to be made like his brothers in every way in order that he might become a merciful and faithful High Priest in service to God. (Heb 2:17)*

Again this is pretty clear. He wasn't just made like us in *some* ways, but in *every* way. The next verse drives the point home even further:

> *Because he himself suffered when he was tempted, he is able to help those who are being tempted. (Heb 2:18)*

He was tempted, and he suffered in the process. Is that how we think of him? A man, struggling against a desire for sin, struggling even though it hurt?

All too often it's easy for us to think of Jesus almost like a machine who was able to do his Father's will automatically, just because he was the son of God. But in fact the scriptures do not say that; rather they say exactly the opposite. Here's an example:

> *Although he was a son, he learned obedience from what he suffered. (Heb 5:8)*

Pause a moment to let this sink in.

Not only was Jesus tempted, and not only did he suffer in that temptation, but he had to learn obedience. That is, Jesus wasn't naturally obedient! It was something he had to learn.

I'm not naturally obedient and neither are you. The scriptures have said that Jesus was made like us in every way — he was not naturally obedient to his Father, either. Instead it was a free choice that he made. As we also can make that choice.

Temptations of Jesus

When we think of the temptation of Jesus, the obvious incident that comes to mind is when he faces temptations during 40 days of fasting in the desert (Luke 4). But I think that this occasion was neither the only period of temptation, nor even the deepest temptation, that Jesus faced.

This incident in the desert, testing though it was, was more of a preparatory period for the most challenging temptations of Jesus. Let us see why. WHAT ARE OURS?

Look at Luke 4:1, for example. The context is that Jesus has just emerged from baptism; he's accepted the idea of being washed and the Holy Spirit has come upon him; he's now imbued with the power of God. A mortal man, *imbued with power of God!*

> *Jesus, full of the Holy Spirit, returned from the Jordan and was led by the Spirit in the desert, where for forty days he was tempted by the devil. (Luke 4:1-2)*

That word *led* is the same word as is elsewhere used of a donkey being led. It's as if Jesus was *drawn* into the wilderness. It wasn't as if the Spirit said: "You might like to go there…"; the Spirit *led* him there.

In Matthew it says,

> *Then Jesus was led by the Spirit into the desert to be tempted by the devil. (Matt 4:1)*

He was led into the desert *in order to be tempted.* So we have this very interesting situation where the Holy Spirit is leading Jesus into the wilderness in order for him to experience temptation.

Why? What is God doing?

It seems that God's purpose is for Jesus to decide how he's going to use the power that has come upon him. He has to confront the real devil of his own desires. Is he going to use the power for himself or for others? Who will be master within Jesus? Flesh, or spirit?

Because Jesus was about to be tempted, the Spirit led him into the wilderness, as the better place to experience and work through the temptations.

This is why he is fasting. He seeks to gain the clarity of mind and spiritual presence that we can get when we go for an extended fast. It is a time of devotion, of prayer, and of self-examination. The various temptations that he faces here are components of working the issue out.

Flesh, or spirit?

The temptations

During his fast — lasting nearly six weeks! — he looks around, and sees stones that remind him of bread. And he's hungry!

It would not be sin to use the power of God to feed himself. But, on the other hand, it is important for Jesus to recognize that physical food isn't the thing he really needs. That, rather, is the word of God.

"I'm not going to use the power of God for satisfying my wish to eat."

He sees the kingdoms of the world in front of him, with the knowledge that he could rule them all if he wished.

Now this isn't a man who is wanting to be a dictator. This is a man who now has the power of God — the power to heal, the power to feed — and he sees the injustice, the intolerance and the violence. He knows that he could do great things. "If I choose my own way, I could bring peace on this earth."

Think what would have happened if he had made that choice. We would read in our history books of a wonderful period about two thousand years ago, centered in Israel. It would be hailed as a Golden Age in the history of the world, where a glorious King reigned peacefully, harmoniously, where injustice was done away with.

But the Golden Age would have lasted only until that man died. Then the bickering and division amongst his followers would have grown, until the world returned to the state that it was in before.

Jesus recognizes that if he follows his own instincts and inclinations, he would not be following his Father. His Father has a plan for recreating the whole of human society, from the inside out, not simply attempting a quick fix.

Flesh or spirit?

"I won't worship the desires of the flesh, I'll worship instead the Lord, my God."

Then, in his mind he goes to Jerusalem, to the highest place on the temple.

He's standing there, imagining himself looking down and seeing the people milling around. He knows that if he casts himself down, God's angels — according to scripture — will guard him carefully, 'They will lift you up in their hands so that you will not strike your foot against a stone' *Then* the people *will* believe! They will believe that I *am* the Messiah!

However, converts gained by outward show are not *true* converts. They are not pricked to their heart, recognizing the emptiness of their present way of life and wanting to go a different way. Oh, it may get converts, but it's not the way to preach.

"Don't test God," he says.

These are the kinds of issues he's working out — for six weeks! How do I use this power that my Father has given me? What kind of man am I to be? What kind of son? Flesh or spirit?

These wilderness temptations gave him time to consider how he ought to react in the confusion of circumstance when he would have little time to think, and when his emotions would be engaged and aroused.

We see an example of this in Nazareth, in the same chapter (Luke 4). Though this incident in Nazareth occurs significantly after the wilderness episode, Luke — as is his practice elsewhere — puts them right next to each other, as if to make a point.

So what happens in Nazareth?

Nazareth

By this stage, Jesus is well into his Capernaum ministry. A lot of preaching, a lot of healing, and now he comes to his home town of Nazareth.

Have they heard stories about him? Are they wondering what kind of man he has grown up to be?

He goes into the synagogue in which he grew up and is surrounded by the people he thinks of as his uncles and aunts, cousins, his brothers and his sisters, his lifelong friends — they're all here. People that he loves.

And he starts teaching them some hard truths...

They become so infuriated by his incisive and inflammatory words that they take him to the brow of the hill upon which the town was built, and are about to throw him down. Leaving aside what could possibly have motivated them to such anger, consider instead the response of Jesus: in the midst of this violent rabble, he turns and walks through the crowd. He walks away.

Years ago, I remember hearing how impressive it was that Jesus had such a presence that somehow he could stare down a crowd, walk right through them, and not allow them to do this to him.

But that's not the *really impressive* thing here. After all, what would have happened if they'd thrown him down?

> *For he will command his angels concerning you to guard you in all your ways; they will lift you up in their hands, so that you will not strike your foot against a stone. (Ps 91:11-12)*

The angels would have intervened. His tempter had quoted this very scripture.

What a way to preach to these people who are not listening to him! "Let them cast me down, and then they will see me for who I really am."

If Jesus had not had the opportunity to work this scenario out in the solitudes of preparation, who knows what choice he would have made?

Who knows whether he would have said, "I'm going to put the Lord to the test. I'm going to let them throw me down. I'm going to see if the angels really will intervene and bear me up!"

Instead, despite the strong motivation and desire to make these people realize who he was, he turned and walked through the crowd, refusing to let them do it to him.

When you are facing temptation, your level of preparation is going to be important. You could come into that situation having thought about it beforehand, prepared yourself for it and decided what the appropriate response would be. Or you could allow yourself to blunder into the situation in the hope that you might be able to cope as best you can. It's your choice.

We know what choice Jesus made.

Summary

Jesus was truly a human being, including having to wrestle with real and forceful temptation. The wilderness temptations came as a preparation for the rigors of the temptations that would arise in life circumstances, as evidenced by the events at Nazareth.

Discussion

1. Discuss the value of fasting during spiritual training.
2. Do you find it hard to think of the temptations of Jesus as real? What implications do you see if they were real, or if they were not?
3. Do you find you are subject to the same kinds of temptation over and over again?

Temptations in life

We've already seen that the devotion and commitment Jesus built with his time in the desert was to be tested in the busyness of real life, but Nazareth wasn't the only time it happened.

Let's look at a couple of other occasions, and build a richer picture of Christ's emotional and spiritual wrestling that the gospels show to us.

Feeding the five thousand

Consider the occasion of the feeding of the five thousand.

Jesus has had a crowd follow him into the wilderness, and stay with him for three days — five thousand men, plus women and children. They are hungry, so he tells the disciples, "We should feed these people because some of them will faint on the way home..."

The miracle is very well known. Jesus directs the people to sit down on the grass, and taking the five loaves and two fish, he looks up to heaven, gives thanks, and shares the bread and the fish.

Enough food is produced for everybody to eat and be satisfied. Indeed, the disciples picked up twelve basketfuls of the broken pieces that were left over.

Then we read:

> *Immediately Jesus made the disciples get into the boat and go on ahead of him to the other side, while he dismissed the crowd. After he had dismissed them, he went up on a mountainside by himself to pray. When evening came, he was there alone. (Matt 14:22-23)*

Why did he make the disciples get into the boat immediately they had finished? Why did he dismiss the crowd? Why did he go into the mountain by himself to pray? What's going on?

Well, John 6 has more details of the same incident that add crucially to our understanding of the occasion. At your leisure, satisfy yourselves that the events of Matthew 14 and John 6 are the same occasion, the same feeding of five thousand.

Here's what John adds:

> *After the people saw the miraculous sign that Jesus did, they began to say, "Surely this is the Prophet who is to come into the world." Jesus, knowing that they intended to come and make him king by force, withdrew again to a mountain by himself. (John 6:14-15)*

That's the missing piece. The reaction of the crowd.

You can imagine the situation. From this paltry amount of food Jesus is able to feed a vast crowd. This would have been shocking, astounding, in this subsistence society where food was always scarce.

"This is the Messiah, this is the King who is to come into the world"

It starts as an occasional comment, a whisper, and then the sound grows as the crowd begins to get excited.

"This could be the establishment of the Kingdom of Israel, the fulfillment of the prophecy!"

"We could get rid of the Romans!"

The disciples would not have been immune. Again we have to imagine their contribution, but it's not hard to do so.

"Master, Master, do you hear what they're saying?! This is your opportunity! This is the chance you've been working towards! You could be King!"

Jesus is *tempted* by this.

How do we know? The wilderness temptation has already demonstrated that this is an idea he wrestles with. Establish the kingdom now? It makes sense — I am the king. He is deeply and sorely tempted. Just let the crowd have their way. He won't even have been the one to do it...

So what does he do?

What do you do when you are tempted by one of the recurring temptations that you face again and again and again and again…?

Jesus takes action.

This situation is too spiritually dangerous for him. Flesh or spirit? It can't be allowed to become even more difficult. Already he is heading towards the limit of his ability to resist.

He takes action. Decisively.

First, Jesus tells his disciples to get into the boat and row to the other side. Now there's a storm coming on that lake. The disciples have fished this lake all their lives. They know this. Row into a growing storm on the Sea of Galilee *at night?!* He says to his disciples, "Get into that boat and go!" "But Master, but there's a storm coming…" *Go!* And they go.

Second, he says to the crowd, "*You* need to go too!" Jesus is not to be dissuaded. This huge crowd is dismissed. No one tries to follow him.

And third, he goes up a mountain by himself and he prays and he prays and he prays. Throughout the night he prays. Father, not my will, but yours be done.

If he hadn't had the courage to do this, if he hadn't had the commitment to righteousness that he exhibits, we wouldn't gather in his name. We wouldn't have this mighty leader, this savior, this insightful judge, this high priest working in the lives of each of us.

Stand in awe of his commitment to righteousness. To right-thinking. To right-doing.

Gethsemane

One more example. Gethsemane.

If there's ever a part of scripture where we should be like Moses and take off our shoes because we're standing on holy ground, it's Gethsemane.

Here our Lord has his heart bared. The turmoil of his spirit is written down for all of us to read, and treat how we will. Will we trample all over it? Or will we approach with caution and humility, astounded that we are privileged to share something so precious and intimate?

If you need to pause to consider your frame of mind as you approach Gethsemane, now is a great time.

We'll follow Matthew's account. Jesus says to the disciples,

> *My soul is overwhelmed with sorrow to the point of death. Stay here and keep watch with me. (Matt 26:38)*

Discounting his use of humorous hyperbole — such as having a plank in the eye! — I don't know of any occasion where Jesus exaggerates concerning himself. It's not his style. So when he says his soul is overwhelmed with sorrow to the point of death, he means it.

"I am so sad I can hardly bear to live. Pray with me."

Going a little further he casts himself down, his face to the ground.

> *My Father, if it is possible, may this cup be taken from me. Yet not as I will, but as you will. (Matt 26:39)*

"Is there any other way, Father? Is there any other way that we can shake the world, that we can show the world what righteousness is? Is there any other way you can perfect *me*, that you can complete the work you are carrying out in me..."

This agony has been with him a long time, maybe for a year or more:

> *I have come to bring fire on the earth and how I wish it were already kindled! But I have a baptism to undergo! How distressed I am until it is completed. (Luke 12:49)*

Distress, tension, turmoil. Now it is reaching breaking point. His prayer takes an hour. Matthew tells us the theme, rather than the words. For an hour he explores two thoughts in prayer: whether a different path is possible; and his commitment to his Father's will.

He returns to his disciples and finds them sleeping. He returns *to us* and *finds us* sleeping. "Could you not keep watch with me for one hour?"

It's not just because *he* needs it. It's because *they* need it. "Peter, you need to keep watch along with me; you need to be praying! Don't you know what you are going to be facing tomorrow? I've told you already, you're going to deny me — and you're sleeping?! Watch and pray so that you will not fall to temptation, for the spirit is willing but the body, the flesh, is weak."

I presume they woke up, but only for a time. They were so tired, so weary.

Jesus went away a second time and prayed.

> *My Father, if it is not possible that this cup be taken away unless I drink it, may your will be done. (Matt 26:42)*

He knows what's happening the following day. He knows he's going to be up there, hung for all to see. He knows that the crowds are going to come past him and mock him, "He could 'save' others, but he can't save himself!"

Oh, but he *could* save himself. He has the power. That makes it harder, because he knows that he will have to resist using that power for hour after hour after hour.

Later on in the garden, Peter will draw his sword and attempt to strike at Judas (I presume), but instead a glancing blow catches the servant of the high priest and cuts off the ear. Jesus says: "Put your sword away!" He says,

> *Do you think I cannot call on my Father, and he will at once put at my disposal more than twelve legions of angels? (Matt 26:53)*

Seventy-two thousand angels! Seventy-two thousand angels on call. For what? To rescue Jesus! If at any time he says, "I don't want to do it!" his Father is ready to rescue him. This is the love and devotion between the Father and his son. This is powerful stuff.

It provides a temptation that is hard to resist.

He came back, and found the disciples sleeping because their eyes were heavy. So he left them and went away once more. He prays a third time, saying the same thing.

> *And being in anguish, he prayed more earnestly, and his sweat was like drops of blood falling to the ground. (Luke 22:44)*

Now we can begin to appreciate Hebrews 2:18, that Jesus suffered when he was tempted.

This is where victory was won. Here at Gethsemane.

At Golgotha, he was hung up to die. Golgotha is where he was able to show the world that the victory had been won. Golgotha was the outward expression of the real victory, a victory that was accomplished here at Gethsemane.

Here at Gethsemane he rejected the natural way. Here he put the devil within him to death. Here he overcame the pressure of the flesh.

Flesh or spirit? He chose spirit.

It's like baptism. Baptism is the outward expression of the change that has already taken place within us. There's nothing magic about going under the water at baptism. It doesn't suddenly make you into a new person — there's no special magic associated with the ceremony. Rather, the commitment takes place *before* baptism, the change of heart that leads us to say, "I want to follow this man, I want to be like him." Baptism is the mark, the demonstration, to the people around you, that says, "I want to be like him, I want to be counted as one of his."

It's like birth. Life doesn't begin the moment the baby is pushed out into the world. Instead life has been growing through the nine months, forming this child, developing the potential it now has. The birth is the fulfillment of the process; the point at which the next stage of life can begin.

It's like marriage, too. Marriage doesn't start at the point you say, "I do." That's when you make the public vows to all those who are around. The decision to marry, the drawing together of two souls, takes place before that. You don't want to get to the point where someone says, "Do you take this man/woman…" and then have to consider what decision to make. It's already made! Now you're making it public.

So it is here. The victory is won. It just remains for the world to realize it too.

When Hebrews says that he learned obedience from what he suffered (Heb 5:8) it isn't just talking about Golgotha. It includes this night before, in Gethsemane, when he is agonizing about the following day — the beatings, the humiliation, the agony — when he works through all of that in his mind the night before, and says, "I still want to obey." Not my will but yours be done.

We see a declaration of the righteousness of Christ. "It is so important for me to serve God that I'll do it even to the point of death. If that means, sometimes, running away from temptation and sin, by saying, 'Disciples, go away! Crowd, go away! Let me get out of this situation and go up the mountain,' then that's what I'll do. If it means spending a night in prayer, agonizing over the temptations I'm going to face tomorrow, then that's what I'll do. And if it means being willing to have my friends and my family reject me, to not realize that I'm the Messiah, then that also is what I'll do."

We see the commitment to righteousness that reaches out to us. It demonstrates what the righteousness of God is like.

We look at him and we say, "I know I fail, and fail repeatedly. But that man — *that man!* That's who I want to be like. I want to be like him."

> *I want to know Christ and the power of his resurrection and the fellowship of sharing in his sufferings, becoming like him in his death, and so, somehow, to attain to the resurrection from the dead. (Phil 3:10-11)*

It doesn't say, "I want to know *about* Christ." It says to *know him.*

I want to know Christ!

Summary

Jesus experienced challenging temptations in the feeding of the 5000, and ultimately at Gethsemane. He faces the temptation head on during that final evening, and his victory over the flesh is won that night.

Discussion

1. What is the difference between temptation and sin? Discuss how it is possible both to struggle with temptation, and yet be without sin. Can you give significant examples in your own life.
2. What do you learn about Jesus from his personal struggle at Gethsemane?
3. In what ways do you think Jesus grew spiritually through his experiences in Gethsemane and Golgotha? Was it too high a price to pay?
4. Open your Bibles to the incident in Matt 14. What does Jesus do after his night in prayer? How much was this enabled by his time of communion with his Father?

In the image of God

Jesus was a man, a human being! He was truly one of us. The same kinds of desires, the same kinds of temptations, the same tiredness, the same frustrations. He was one of us!

There was no magic in him that made him sinless, no miracle cure that wiped out the daily struggle against sin. He was just like you. Just like me. Yet he became living proof that it is possible for a human being to be sinless.

I've heard some Christians claim that Jesus' temptations were symbolic rather than real, who say, "I know Jesus was tempted, but he couldn't actually have sinned."

But that's not the picture we've already seen from Scripture.

Rather we see a human son, conceived of the spirit, born just like us, and nurtured by his Father, trained and perfected by his Father, throughout the whole of his life. As a human child he devoted himself to pleasing his Father. As an adult, he lived a sinless life, not because he was not subject to human weakness, but because of his lifelong commitment to the training and discipline of the Father, to the intimacy of the relationship between them.

Listen to Hebrews again:

> *During the days of Jesus' life on earth, he offered up prayers and petitions with loud cries and tears to the one who could save him from death, and he was heard because of his reverent submission. Although he was a son, he learned obedience from what he suffered and, once made perfect, he became the source of eternal salvation for all who obey him (Heb 5:7-9).*

Jesus Christ, a man. A man who wanted to avoid death, like all of us! He pleaded with his Father in heaven to see if there was an alternative path, to see if there was a way that did not involve Golgotha. Yet there was not.

Although he was a son he learned obedience.

Obedience doesn't come naturally to me, and this passage says that it didn't come naturally to Jesus, either. He prayed extensively in three periods of prayer for the spirit to overcome the flesh. And he won the battle within himself through the strength God provided.

Jesus had to learn to obey, and he had to be "perfected", or as it says above, "made perfect." The Greek here doesn't imply that Jesus was flawed, but rather that he was incomplete.

> *In bringing many sons to glory, it was fitting that God, for whom and through whom everything exists, should make the author of their salvation perfect through suffering. (Heb 2:10)*

He was *untarnished,* but he was also *unfinished.* The love he shared with his Father was so powerful, so strong, that it continued to carry the two of them through this whole process, through the rigors of Christ's development and nurturing, so that he could come out the other side of the experience as one in whom the word of God was fully embodied, in every aspect, in every dimension.

And once his training was completed, he became the source of eternal salvation for all who obey him.

Human nature

There is a view among many Christians that human beings are fundamentally flawed, that our flesh is inherently evil. Jeremiah is certainly clear that our natural human orientation is away from God:

> *The heart is deceitful above all things and beyond cure. Who can understand it? (Jer 17:9)*

Note that this doesn't say that our flesh, our physical nature is somehow intrinsically sullied. Rather, it emphasizes that we have a drive within us to deceive and distort. Jeremiah does not comment here about whether that tendency can be overcome.

Jesus was human, and didn't sin. He was just like you. Just like me. Yet he is proof that through the strength of God it is possible for a human being to overcome temptation and live a holy life.

> *It is God's will that you should be sanctified (1 Thess 4:3)*

I think there's a danger if we assume that our mortal frame cannot be holy. I have heard Christians excuse their destructive acts with, "It's just human nature," as if that somehow makes it okay, or excusable. "We are just human, so of course I get to do destructive things."

But this is in direct opposition to the call of Scripture:

> *We know that we have come to know him if we obey his commands. The man who says, "I know him," but does not do what he commands is a liar, and the truth is not in him. But if anyone obeys his word, God's love is truly made complete in him. This is how we know we are in him: Whoever claims to live in him must walk as Jesus did. (1 John 2:3-6)*

and even more challenging:

> *But you know that he appeared so that he might take away our sins. And in him is no sin. No one who lives in him keeps on sinning. No one who continues to sin has either seen him or known him. (1 John 3:5-6)*

Now, neither of these passages are teaching that we are saved by works. But they are making it very clear that the disciple should expect to be transformed, and should have put a life of sin into the past. The spirit and attitude of the Lord Jesus should reign in the heart of his follower. No doubt we each have all sorts of pressures and challenges, but how we respond to them is a reflection of our heart — a mirror of the soul.

In the form of God

Jesus was one of us. But that's not all that can be said about him:

> *Who, being in very nature God, did not consider equality with God something to be grasped, but made himself nothing, taking the very nature of a servant, being made in human likeness. (Phil 2:6-7).*

I think these verses are often misunderstood, as if Paul is drawing a contrast between God-nature and human-nature. Let me be bold: that's sloppy reading. The contrast Paul is actually drawing is between being God-like and servant-like. It is not whether Jesus was immortal or mortal, but whether he was by nature a ruler or a slave.

There are echoes with what was said to Moses 1500 years previously:

> *Then the LORD said to Moses, "See, I have made you like God to Pharaoh, and your brother Aaron will be your prophet. (Ex 7:1)*

Moses had become like God in that his word became absolute. He had become God-like, at least as far as Pharaoh was concerned. If Moses called for darkness, there was darkness. If he called for frogs, there were frogs. Whatever he declared, it came to pass. This is just like God himself:

> *... so is my word that goes out from my mouth: It will not return to me empty, but will accomplish what I desire and achieve the purpose for which I sent it. (Is 55:11)*

This was the natural state of Jesus from the start. Though completely human, he was born King of the World, the Heir to the Universe. By the nature of his inheritance, whatever he spoke, whatever thing he declared, would have come to pass. The wise magi recognized this, and though he was barely a year old at the time, brought him gifts as befitted a ruler: gold, frankincense, and myrrh.

As heir he could have demanded to live in palaces, to live a life of luxury. As heir he could retreat from the world and make proclamations from on high. He could have taken, outwardly, the form of God — ruler, awesomely mighty. But he didn't.

Instead, he emptied himself. He made himself nothing, and took on himself absolute servanthood, the nature of slavery. He was the servant of everyone he saw; whether reaching out to the crowds of people who followed him even when he was exhausted, or choosing to wash his disciples feet in such a blatant act of servitude that Peter was embarrassed (John 13:6-8).

In reality, Jesus became the total servant because that's who God is: the provider of all, the shepherd to all.

> *He tends his flock like a shepherd: He gathers the lambs in his arms and carries them close to his heart; he gently leads those that have young. (Is 40:11)*

Paul continues his description about Jesus:

> *And being found in appearance as a man, he humbled himself and became obedient to death – even death on a cross! Therefore God*

> *exalted him to the highest place and gave him the name that is above every name. (Phil 2:8-9)*

He made himself helpless in death. He had no power in himself. Instead, it was complete dependence on his Father. Total trust.

Notice it was not simply that Jesus died when God told him to. Paul's phrasing suggests much more. Jesus' *life* was a life of obedience and submission to his Father; he became *obedient throughout his life*, even to the point of death, and even to the point of death on a cross!

This is the same observation that we made much earlier, that Jesus' death was the culmination of his life, and not some event separated from it. His life was the symphony, his death was the finale of the piece. (His resurrection then opened up a new and even more dramatic overture.)

And throughout Jesus' life he learned obedience. Think about that.

Jesus knows how to obey his Father, how to obey God absolutely, to the ultimate. There is no deeper test. His training had reached the point of completion. Jesus' will and choice now resonate perfectly with his Father's will and choice. By being servant, he learned truly and deeply how to be ruler.

So God exalts him to the highest place.

His son, the man Jesus, has grown to reflect the wisdom, the righteousness, and the love of God himself, fully and without reservation. Therefore God gives him the name that is above every name.

This is why we should bow at the name of Jesus, why every knee should bow, in heaven and on earth and under the earth.

Consider this. Moses was a mighty prophet and we ought to be humble before him. Abraham likewise was an outstanding example of faith, and we ought similarly to be humble before him. Yet Jesus makes those two men pale into insignificance. So great and awesome, he stands far, far above the accomplishments of these and other noteworthy spiritual men and women.

Indeed, both Moses and Abraham will bow before him and worship him as the one who manifests God to us.

This is what he accomplished: he and the Father, working together. This is mightiness! This is God manifested in the flesh!

When Philip says to him: "Show us the Father and that'll be good enough for us!" Jesus answers,

> *Don't you know me, Philip, even after I have been among you such a long time? Anyone who has seen me has seen the Father. How can you say, 'Show us the Father'? (John 14:9)*

Paraphrasing his response, Jesus is saying, "Don't you realize that I've been showing you the Father? Everything that I've been doing has been expressing to you what God is like. I have only been doing those things that demonstrate the Father to you!"

I don't know if he was exasperated, but he certainly seems to be astonished that Philip hadn't already figured that out.

Word of God

This accomplishment of the Father and Son together fulfilled the prophecy of Isaiah from hundreds of years earlier.

> *"The virgin will be with child and will give birth to a son, and they will call him Immanuel"—which means, "God with us."*
> *(Matt 1:23)*

The purpose of Jesus is not to be an alternative to God, but rather he brings God's presence among us. As God declares:

> *I will put my words in his mouth. (Deut 18:18)*

From the very start, all the things Jesus said were the words of God — more, he was the very embodiment of the word of God.

Everything God ever did was done through his word. Right from the beginning, "God said" and then it happened. Just three verses into the Bible:

> *God said, "Let there be light," and there was light. (Gen 1:3)*

The Psalms emphasize this point:

> *By the word of the LORD were the heavens made, their starry host by the breath of his mouth. (Ps 33:6)*

I think this is what John is referring to at the start of his gospel:

> *In the beginning was the Word, and the Word was with God, and the Word was God. He was with God in the beginning. Through him all things were made; without him nothing was made that has been made. (John 1:1-3)*

Even though our English translations use the words *he* and *him*, the original is just as well translated with *it.* Here's my best effort at a much more literal translation of what John wrote:

> *In the beginning was the word, and the word was oriented to God, and what God was, the word was. It was in the beginning oriented to God. Through it all things were made; and without it not one thing was made that has been made.*

There is no difference between who God is, and what he declares through his word. God uses his word to declare every creative act that he performs. God declares something, and it comes to be.

> *As the rain and the snow come down from heaven, and do not return to it without watering the earth and making it bud and flourish, so that it yields seed for the sower and bread for the eater, so is my word that goes out from my mouth: It will not return to me empty, but will accomplish what I desire and achieve the purpose for which I sent it. (Is 55:10-11)*

God's word, creating, nurturing, guiding. And now, that creative word of God has been embodied in a man.

> *The word became flesh and made his dwelling among us (John 1:14).*

If you look at the context, John is clearly referring to Jesus here. The word of God was made flesh — the Greek word for *became* is the same one translated *made* in John 1:3 above.

I like to think of the Bible as *the word of God made paper.* So Jesus is *the word of God made flesh.* He is the embodiment of the word of God. Everything God has been saying is encapsulated in this man.

We get a very similar claim at the start of Hebrews:

> *In the past God spoke to our forefathers through the prophets at many times and in various ways, but in these last days he has spoken to us by his Son (Heb 1:1-2)*

Jesus, says the writer here, is God talking to us.

In earlier times, God spoke through many other prophets. We read explicitly of *the word of the LORD* coming to Abraham, Moses, Samuel, Nathan, Gad, Solomon, Ahijah, Jehu, Elijah, Isaiah, Jeremiah, Jonah, Haggai, Micah, Zephaniah, and so on. God was speaking to each of these people, for them to share the word with us. And now, God has spoken to us by his Son.

God's word, embodied in a man!

After Jesus' resurrection and ascension into heaven, the New Testament writers attest to how completely he embodies God's intent by declaring the *Word of God* as a name and title of Jesus:

> *His eyes are like blazing fire, and on his head are many crowns. He has a name written on him that no one knows but he himself. He is dressed in a robe dipped in blood, and his name is the Word of God. (Rev 19:12-13)*

Everything God has been saying, everything he has been trying to accomplish, all that God is and does, is manifest in Jesus Christ.

Another way of saying the same thing is that he is the *image* of God:

> *He is the image of the invisible God, the firstborn over all creation. (Col 1:15)*

The son of Mary, a human child conceived by the holy spirit, he grew and struggled and matured until ultimately he was perfected by the Father's work in his life. He shows us the Father. He embodies everything God has ever been saying.

In passing, I wonder if the following passage is also referring to Jesus:

> *For the word of God is living and active. Sharper than any double-edged sword, it penetrates even to dividing soul and spirit, joints and marrow; it judges the thoughts and attitudes of the heart. Nothing in all creation is hidden from God's sight. Everything is uncovered and laid bare before the eyes of him to whom we must give account. (Heb 4:12-13)*

I had always previously thought this passage was referring to the scriptures, the written word of God. But as we have seen, the Greek doesn't always distinguish well between *he* and *it*. If we reread these verses with *he*, they have an extra power as possibly describing the embodied word of God, Jesus the savior, Jesus the judge.

The perfect man

Not all human beings are equivalent in every way. Some of us are stronger than others, or taller, or smarter, or faster. Others are kinder, or more compassionate, or fairer. Yet others are wiser, or more insightful. We are not the same as each other, but we are all human.

Having God as his father didn't make Jesus any less human. Rather, it allowed him to become as wonderful as a human can be. He shows us what we can aspire to. He is like us, so we can relate to him, but he is so beyond us that we can never outgrow him. He is the pinnacle of spirituality.

He was human, but he was a unique human. As we will see later, he was the first to be completed in the image of God.

Summary

Jesus is the human manifestation of everything God is and says. But it didn't come to him for free: he underwent his own personal discipline, and was perfected in the process. He is in the image of God. He is the word of God.

Discussion

1. Does it come as a surprise that Jesus needed training and personal discipline?
2. Can you think of any occasions in Jesus' life that show him growing spiritually?
3. What spiritual training do you have in your life?

Savior Judge

Jesus is Savior. He is also Judge. Listen to what Paul tells the people of Athens:

> *For [God] has set a day when he will judge the world with justice by the man he has appointed. He has given proof of this to all men by raising him from the dead. (Acts 17:31)*

I think it is significant that, not only is Jesus helping and supporting us as our savior, but is also assessing whether we are meeting the standard his Father has set.

We touched on this topic of standards earlier when we discussed the constraint triangles. Because God wants to make a loving community of people who exercise their freewill, we have to choose whether we want to be part of it or not.

The work of Jesus is to encourage us, to draw us in, to help us to want to be part of a community of love, and to give us the ability to participate in one.

At the same time, Jesus is continually looking deep into our hearts to see if we really do want healing and righteousness or not. As he said to a man who had been ill for 38 years:

> *Do you want to get well? (John 5:6)*

He asks the same question of each one of us.

It's only because Jesus can see where we are lacking something that he's able to step in to try to build that aspect of our character. Or to put it another way, if Jesus couldn't tell whether we loved one another or not, for example, he couldn't do much to help develop our love.

Imagine taking parachuting lessons. You wouldn't want your instructor to be teaching you and not notice that you keep forgetting about this "ripcord thing." You want the instructor to see every shortcoming, and to help you overcome. Even at the end, it makes no sense for the instructor to say, "Oh well, never mind about the ripcord! I pass all my students anyway!" and you end up jumping into thin air. Disaster!

You see, there are some things that have intrinsic requirements — you really want to know how to parachute before someone passes you on the test!

It's the same with salvation. I wouldn't want to be in the kingdom if, when Christ comes and looks closely into my heart, he finds that it's not what I really want. If Christ knows that deep down I would resent and rebel against the kind of loving community that the Father is building, then the kingdom would be "hell" for me. The oblivion of death would be an act of mercy.

These two familiar ideas both apply to Jesus, that of a savior and that of a judge. These two roles represent the two sides of his work with us.

Why Jesus?

We've seen that because of our deep-rooted and visceral fear of God, he has always worked through intermediaries to draw people to him. Through the ages it has been the same. God has appointed prophets, priests, and judges to represent him, to act as saviors to his people. In many cases they were effective, turning many from sin.

Yet in the end, God had to send Jesus.

Why?

To be fully effective, God's intermediary needs fully to reflect God's character and attributes, or else God cannot place full trust and authority in him or her.

Unfortunately, even the best of God's prophets were distorted by sin and their sinful acts.

Look through Biblical history and you will see the pattern repeated. Abraham lied twice about his true relationship with Sarah. Moses dishonored God when he overstepped his instructions and struck the rock twice. Samson could not resist the sexual attraction of women.

And Samuel, a great man, a great judge, and yet... Just pause for a moment and consider the fact that he didn't really notice what his sons were doing. They went after dishonest gain, they accepted bribes, and they perverted justice (1 Sam 8:3), yet he did nothing about it. Instead, God's name become defamed among the people. Even a mighty man like Samuel is diminished in his capacity to act as the voice of God on earth.

Or David. He would have been a wonderful savior and judge, except that the last part of his life was horribly damaged by the terrible effects associated "with the matter of Uriah the Hittite" (2 Kings 15:5). His sin, from stealing another man's wife, to engaging in murder in a vain attempt at cover up, affected him so profoundly.

That sin of David distorted his message, weakened his leadership, and diminished his capacity to bring the judgment of God among the people. Not only did the people think less of him afterwards, but he was less willing to call out sin on God's behalf.

It is one thing for God to send a prophet who is a human being, just like us, someone we can relate to in order to encourage and reassure us. It is significantly another thing to find a man who is just like God in his character, so that he's able to give correct judgment, and able to express the will of God in the judgment that he gives. To accomplish that means the person must have no flaws in saying or doing, in thinking or feeling, in choices or in purpose.

The ultimate savior judge has to be sinless.

Throughout his life Jesus was wrestling against sin; against the same temptations that you and I struggle with, temptations that could have led him astray, that could have damaged him as badly as our sin damages us.

What if he had succumbed?

Since the temptations were real, then there was a real possibility that he might have chosen his own path, his own desires, rather than the path his Father had laid out for him. So, what if he had succumbed?

I think he would still have been a mighty, mighty man. He would have been like a Daniel or a Moses, but even greater. He would have left wisdom and inspiration to countless human beings after him. He would have been a towering example of faith and spirituality.

Yet for all that, he would also have been a man unfit for the awesome task towards which his Father was training, disciplining, and nurturing him: to be the very voice of God amongst us. His sin would have introduced a discordant note, and God could not have entrusted all judgment to his care.

But he didn't succumb!

Instead, he overcame! Completely, totally, and utterly.

Jesus has been trained, he has been nurtured, he has been perfected. He is truly the manifestation of God in the flesh, taking on the divine nature. Consequently, and this is the fundamental principle that we need to take away, Christ is able to save and to judge.

He started as just one of us. But now, in every way possible, the Father is in him and he is in the Father — every element of the word of God is now expressed through him.

> *He is the image of the invisible God, the firstborn over all creation. (Col 1:15)*

In Genesis, when God said, "Let us make man in our image," I don't think he was talking just about a single act long ago. I think he was declaring his creative work through the ages, when he is creating men and women to be like him. God's work has always been to manifest himself in living beings, to create us to be in his image.

Jesus is the first man to be perfectly completed in the image of God. At his resurrection, the creative work of his Father was finished as far as his son was concerned. His son, one of us, but also fully in the image of God, and so worthy to receive the authority of his Father.

Jesus, the Savior Judge

Soon after Pentecost, the apostles Peter and John are hauled before the Sanhedrin, the religious ruling council, and are told not to preach in the name of Jesus. Listen to what Peter says about Jesus:

> *God exalted him to his own right hand as Prince and Savior that he might give repentance and forgiveness of sins to Israel. (Acts 5:31)*

God has exalted him to authority. Moreover, he is both Prince (i.e., judge) and Savior. As Savior, he leads us to repentance, so that we turn from our sin. As Prince, his authority to forgive is matched by his authority not to forgive. That's what 'judgment' is. Christ's ability to forgive is balanced by his authority to condemn.

Remember the salvation process we considered previously? These were the phases we identified:

- God declares our sin and proclaims his love;
- We agree and want to be different;
- He forgives us and liberates us from our guilt;
- We trust in his forgiveness and participate in his work of making us different;
- He completes the work that he does in this life through resurrection and judgment.

Jesus is part of every one of these steps!

He is part of the declaration of our sin, and he's certainly part of the declaration of God's love for us, as John 3:16 states.

Through his example, Jesus encourages us to want to be different. We see him and are inspired: "That is the man I want to be like!"

He forgives; he liberates us from our guilt. He's the one to whom the Father has entrusted this authority:

> *... know that the Son of Man has authority on earth to forgive sins (Matt 9:6)*

In response, we trust in him! We trust in his ability and willingness to work in our lives, to guide us, to have the angels on hand when we need help, when we need strength. The fact that he is like us helps to give us the courage to go to the heavenly throne to find grace and mercy, to help us in our time of need.

And, of course, he is the one who will be calling us out from the grave. He's been appointed to this role by the Father because he reflects and manifests the Father.

He is key to every phase of our salvation.

With his authority and mighty power, he will bring to fulfillment the Father's creative work of making multitudes of people in the image of God.

> *... you have taken off your old self with its practices and have put on the new self, which is being renewed in knowledge in the image of its Creator. (Col 3:9-10)*

Peter expresses the same idea as *sharing in the divine nature*:

> *Through these he has given us his very great and precious promises, so that through them you may participate in the divine nature and escape the corruption in the world caused by evil desires. (1 Pet 1:4)*

At the resurrection we also will be manifestations of God! It's a tremendous hope! Christ is the firstfruits, blazing the trail for us to follow.

> *And we, who with unveiled faces all reflect the Lord's glory, are being transformed into his likeness with ever-increasing glory... (2 Cor 3:18)*

When God finally rests, when Christ has completed his work as Savior Judge, when death is destroyed at last, God will stand back and survey the work he has accomplished.

> *God saw all that he had made, and it was very good. (Gen 1:31)*

I read this as a prophecy. Right at the beginning of Genesis, we are given a vision of the whole of the creative work that God is accomplishing with us.

Summary

Through the disciplines of his life, Jesus came to manifest God perfectly. Consequently, he has been appointed as savior and judge on God's behalf. He is entrusted with every aspect of the salvation process, fulfilling God's will in rescuing us from death.

Discussion

1. Are Jesus' dual roles of savior and judge in conflict with one another, or are they mutually supporting? Try to find some examples in everyday life.
2. Is there any sense in which we are supposed to reflect Jesus' dual role as savior judge?

3. What if the savior judge had been born with a human father? Would that have interfered with his ability to be fully unbiased in judgment?

The present work of Jesus

The Bible tells us that Jesus ascended to heaven after his resurrection, and that he now sits on the Father's throne, at God's right hand.

So what is he doing there?

Is he just waiting until the day comes for him to return to the world in power? Or does he have work to do in the present age?

Most Christians will probably say that Jesus has a role as an intermediary between ourselves and God, in that he takes our prayers and presents them to the Father. Many might go on to say that he pleads our cause (when we ask for forgiveness), that he adjusts our prayers (when we don't know what to pray for, or how to express ourselves adequately), and that Jesus presents our case to God, seeks forgiveness for us so that we may be reconciled to God.

If pressed further, some would draw the parallel with Moses pleading to God to give Israel another chance and God responding and relenting from the destruction he had planned. Jesus gets placed in a similar role: he is greater than Moses, and he is now exalted to God's right hand, and it makes a kind of sense that he intercedes with God on our behalf.

But is all this correct? Is this a Biblical view?

As we've seen a number of times already, it is by asking these kinds of questions that we are able to open up some of the richness that we might otherwise miss in scripture.

Challenging the traditional intercession role

There are a number of passages that appear to support a traditional view of Jesus as our intercessor before God. For example:

> *Now there have been many of those priests, since death prevented them from continuing in office; but because Jesus lives forever, he*

> *has a permanent priesthood. Therefore he is able to save completely those who come to God through him, because he always lives to intercede for them. (Heb 7:23-25)*

At first sight, it looks like Jesus goes into God's temple in heaven, and intercedes with God on our behalf.

However, there are a number of other scriptures that seriously challenge this traditional perspective. We'll look at three in turn, and then step back to see what we should make of it all. Let me warn you ahead of time: this is another unraveling chapter, and it may make us uncomfortable for a while.

Jesus rejects being a go-between

We begin with Jesus himself. Astonishingly (to me at least) Jesus says that it is *not* his role to be a go-between in the way commonly understood.

> *In that day you will ask in my name. I am not saying that I will ask the Father on your behalf. No, the Father himself loves you because you have loved me and have believed that I came from God. (John 16:26-27)*

The context is that the last supper has just taken place. Jesus and his disciples have left the upper room and are walking through the streets of Jerusalem, towards the outskirts of the city where he is about to offer his extended prayer (in John 17), before crossing the Kidron en route to the garden of Gethsemane. It is in this very urgent and tense situation that he revealed this to them.

Let's paraphrase it: "Don't think," he says, "when you pray in my name that I will be taking your message to the Father. It's not like that at all. You will be able to deal directly with the Father. He loves you, because you have loved me and believed in me."

So that's the first challenge: Jesus says he will not be in the role of an intermediary in our prayers. We can pray to the Father directly.

Jesus has authority himself

Here's a second challenge. Remember the incident in Jesus' ministry when the paralytic was let down through the roof of the house? There he was, lying on the floor at Jesus' feet, unable to move. Jesus says to him "Son, your sins are forgiven." The Pharisees said he was speaking blasphemy — no one can forgive sins but God alone. Jesus' response is definitive.

> *Which is easier: to say, 'Your sins are forgiven,' or to say, 'Get up and walk'? But that you may know that the Son of Man has authority on earth to forgive sins...' he said to the paralyzed man, 'I tell you, get up, take your mat and go home.' Immediately he stood up in front of them, took what he had been lying on and went home praising God. (Luke 5:23-25)*

The man took up his bed and walked out, healed and forgiven!

What was the one lesson Jesus wanted us all to learn from this? It was this: that he *personally had the authority to forgive sin!*

Now all this was *before* his death and resurrection. Do we seriously imagine that our Lord has any *less* authority now, seated at God's right hand? He himself says,

> *All authority in heaven and on earth has been given to me. (Matt 28:18)*

Our Lord, who had authority to forgive sins in the days of his flesh, has all that authority and more in his glorified state. Stephen knows this. In his final moment, as the stones are being hurled, he prays to Jesus to forgive those who are murdering him.

> *While they were stoning him, Stephen prayed, "Lord Jesus, receive my spirit." Then he fell on his knees and cried out, "Lord, do not hold this sin against them." When he had said this, he fell asleep. (Acts 7:59-60)*

So then, as Jesus already has the authority to forgive, why would he need to go to the Father and say, "Please forgive their sins, for my sake" when he has that power himself? It just doesn't make sense.

Jesus reflects the Father perfectly

There's a third challenge to consider. This one comes from a principle discussed just before Jesus leaves the upper room of the last supper.

> *Philip said, 'Lord, show us the Father and that will be enough for us.' Jesus answered: 'Don't you know me, Philip, even after I have been among you such a long time? Anyone who has seen me has*

> *seen the Father. How can you say, 'Show us the Father'? Don't you believe that I am in the Father, and that the Father is in me? The words I say to you are not just my own. Rather, it is the Father, living in me, who is doing his work. (John 14:8-10)*

Jesus' reply to Philip's request is, "Don't you realize what I have been doing for the past three and a half years, Philip? I *have been* showing you the Father. Everything I have been saying and doing has been designed to reveal my Father to you."

This was the whole tenor of Jesus' life, as we've already examined in some detail. His life was devoted to reflecting what the Father would feel about *this* situation, or what he would do or say in *that* situation, and then acting accordingly. "I do only those things which I have seen of my Father, which I have learned of my Father, which the Father has taught me," and so on.

This is what Jesus' life was all about: he was completely attuned to his Father's will. So here in John 14 he says, "If you want to know what God is like, look at me!"

If ever we want to know how *loving* God is, we should look at Jesus and see when he showed love, and kindness, and compassion.

If ever we want to know how *concerned* God is about our salvation, we should look at Jesus grieving that the people are as sheep without a shepherd, and doing everything possible to meet their needs.

If ever we want to know how *angry* God can be, we should look at Jesus, and see the fire blazing within as he makes a whip and cleanses the temple. We look to the Son, because he displays the Father in all the dimensions of the Father's character.

But this means that Jesus is neither more strict, nor more lenient than the Father. He makes exactly the same judgment calls as his Father!

> *The Father judges rightly, for he is righteous and true altogether. (Ps 145:17)*

So how could the Father possibly give all judgment to the Son if the Son were to come to different conclusions? It is only because the Son is perfectly attuned to the will of the Father that he has been appointed judge of heaven and earth.

Of necessity, though, this means that there is no occasion where God would want to forgive and the Son would not, nor vice versa. If Jesus wants to forgive, then that's because it's the right thing to do. So how could there be a situation where Jesus would need to plead our cause to the Father?

We need to read carefully

These are three serious challenges to the common view that Jesus takes our prayers to the Father and presents our case to God. To summarize:

- Jesus says explicitly that he won't be this 'middleman' between us and the Father. We can pray directly to the Father.
- He also says, and demonstrated in his ministry, that he personally had the authority to forgive sins. It was true then. It is still true now.
- He goes to great lengths to demonstrate that he is perfectly in tune with his Father's will. There is no conflict or debate between them whether it would or would not be appropriate to forgive sins.

So what do we make of this?

I dare say many readers may be uncomfortable at this point. Again, I encourage you to bear with me. After all, apparent Scriptural conflicts are quite common: when you read one passage it seems to say one thing, and when you read another it seems to say something contradictory. This is exactly the situation we find ourselves in now.

What do we do when we come across these apparent conflicts?

We dig deeper.

We compare and contrast multiple passages and look for what the weight of Scripture is really telling us. In my experience, every time we do this, the apparent contradictions evaporate so long as we are prepared to give up our preconceived ideas and understanding. Moreover, not only do the contradictions evaporate, but the truths we discover in the process are far richer than the conceptions we had previously.

So let us pause at this point, before resolving the issue, and be aware of the challenge posed by the words from the spirit.

Summary

The popular idea that Jesus is interceding with God on our behalf runs into many problems when it is examined in detail. Jesus himself denies that this is his role, and it is inconsistent with who he is, and with the authorities that have already been granted to him.

Discussion

1. Prior to reading this section, what was your understanding of the present work of Jesus? What is he doing today?
2. Can you think of any passages that supported (or seemed to support) your prior view? List them out so that you can make sure not to forget about them later.
3. Which of the arguments presented here did you find compelling (if any)?
4. Discuss together how it feels when you find some of your beliefs or understandings challenged.

Jesus as mediator

In the last section, we presented some challenges to the widespread teaching in Christianity that Christ's present work in heaven is to intercede with God on our behalf. In this section, we will seek to find a resolution to apparent contradictions we have uncovered.

Biases in translations

As we reexamine the relevant scriptures, we must take care lest we unwittingly allow ourselves to be influenced by our background assumptions. In this case we have an extra challenge, because we have also to wrestle with the bias of the translators of the Bible.

Let me give you an example. Consider a passage in 1 John. First read the RSV (the KJV is similar).

> *My little children, I am writing this to you so that you may not sin; but if any one does sin, we have an advocate with the Father, Jesus Christ the righteous; (1 John 2:1)*

This is pretty close to the Greek original. Perhaps the choice of the word 'advocate' could suggest someone arguing our case in a legal context, which I will later suggest is not quite right.

But the NIV goes overboard. This is what it says:

> *My dear children I write this to you so that you will not sin. But if anyone does sin, we have one who speaks to the Father in our defense, Jesus Christ the Righteous One.*

Now that's not translating the Greek text. It's adding whole concepts under the guise of dynamic equivalence. The whole phrase "one who speaks … in our defense" is an interpretation that has been inserted as if it is in the text itself. The NIV, though a marvelous translation in so many ways, is here reflecting the doctrinal bias of its scholarship.

So what does the verse actually say? The word translated *'advocate'* by the RSV is the word *parakletos,* the same word Jesus uses in John 14 when he describes the *'comforter'* or *'counselor'* he is going to send them to help them. Literally the word *'parakletos'* simply means *helper*, and that is exactly the sense it has in John 14. To make this clear, just imagine going back into John 14, and repeatedly inserting the phrase "one who speaks to the Father in our defense" every time Jesus talks about the comforter being there to support the disciples. You would soon get the idea that it doesn't make sense.

So taking the translation of *parakletos* to be *helper*, the verse we were considering (1 John 2:1) is simply telling us "if any one does sin, we have a *helper* with the Father, Jesus Christ the righteous." This accords with Jesus' own teaching in John 14:18, where he states that the *parakletos* is his own spiritual presence coming among them*. But we are getting ahead of ourselves. For the moment our purpose is simply to demonstrate the kind of doctrinal bias that can creep into our thinking with a little help from the translators, *i.e.* that we have "one who speaks to the Father in our defense." That is *not* what the Greek text says.

Mediator

So let's return to our main point: the role of Jesus today.

Let's think about Jesus as mediator. Now I've been quite careful in my words. I didn't use the phrase "Jesus our mediator" even though it is in popular usage, because, surprisingly enough, it is actually *not* a Biblical phrase, at least not quite.

The Bible at no point describes Jesus as *'our'* mediator. Rather, Jesus is always presented to us as a mediator sent by God, and in particular, as the mediator of the new covenant. As we will see, this makes a considerable difference.

To convince ourselves of this Biblical usage we'll look at all the passages in the New Testament that mention *mediator*. There are only five of them.

We start with Paul's first letter to Timothy:

---

* *Perhaps in the form of the "Angel of the Presence" referred to elsewhere in the Bible.*

> *... God our Savior, who wants all men to be saved and to come to a knowledge of the truth. For there is one God and one mediator between God and men, the man Christ Jesus, who gave himself as a ransom for all men — the testimony given in its proper time. And for this purpose I was appointed a herald and an apostle ...*
> *(1 Tim 2:3-7)*

In this passage Paul starts with the idea of God being our savior. This is a fundamental truth which we've examined already. God *is* the one who saves us. He is our *Savior*. It is by extension that the Lord Jesus is also our Savior, because he is a manifestation of the Father and was instrumental in carrying out God's plan. Salvation starts with God.

Given this context, look at what the 'mediator' did. He gave himself as a testimony, given at the proper time. To whom was he testifying? To God, or to humanity? As soon as we ask the question the answer is obvious. God didn't need the testimony. We did. Christ Jesus was testifying to humanity.

The whole thrust of this passage is: *from* God, *to* humanity.

God, the author of salvation, is working through Christ to bring the knowledge of the truth to men and women. That work then continues through the apostles who take it from Christ, and continue his work. Throughout all this, the direction is from God to humanity. Jesus is the appointed mediator of that message of truth and salvation.

In everyday speech we speak of 'a medium of instruction,' or 'the media,' meaning TV, radio and newspapers. The medium is the channel through which a message flows. The message is *mediated* through the channel.

So it is here. Jesus is the medium through which God speaks to us. He is the *mediator* of the message, which was the ransom, the testimony.

Again, note the direction. We did not pick Jesus as our representative to talk to God. Not at all! It is entirely the other way round. God has appointed Jesus as *his* representative to reach out and communicate with us.

Same idea in Hebrews

Most of the other passages about 'mediator' occur in Hebrews. Here's the first.

> *How much more, then, will the blood of Christ, who through the eternal Spirit offered himself unblemished to God, cleanse our consciences from acts that lead to death, so that we may serve the living God! For this reason Christ is the mediator of a new covenant, that those who are called may receive the promised eternal inheritance – now that he has died as a ransom to set them free from the sins committed under the first covenant. (Heb 9:14-15)*

Look at the sense in which Christ is mediator. He is the 'mediator' of the new covenant.

Where does that covenant come from? Did we come up with the idea? Of course not! It was God's idea. He developed the plan, and he sent Christ to bring the glad message to us. Christ mediates the new covenant, bringing it from God to us.

We have exactly the same teaching and emphasis a couple of chapters later.

> *But you have come to Mount Zion, to the heavenly Jerusalem, the city of the living God. You have come to thousands upon thousands of angels in joyful assembly, to the church of the firstborn, whose names are written in heaven. You have come to God, the judge of all men, to the spirits of righteous men made perfect, to Jesus the mediator of a new covenant, and to the sprinkled blood that speaks a better word than the blood of Abel. (Heb 12:22-24)*

Again, the Lord Jesus is *God's* mediator, bringing the covenant to us. He is not *our* mediator, appointed to present our case to God. That idea is completely absent from these verses. The direction is from God to man.

The situation under the Old Testament was directly parallel. Moses wasn't chosen by Israel to present their case to God. Quite the reverse. God chose Moses as *his* representative, gave him the ten commandments and the words of the covenant on Sinai, and Moses then had to present it all to the people. He had to 'mediate' the covenant between God and man. The direction was the same. And this is the point of the final occurrences of the mediator word in the New Testament.

> *What, then, was the purpose of the law? It was added because of transgressions until the Seed to whom the promise referred had*

> *come. The law was put into effect through angels by a mediator. A mediator, however, does not represent just one party; but God is one. (Gal 3:19-20)*

The main point of these verses is just like in Hebrews. The law came from God to humanity and a mediator was engaged to transmit this message. Moses was God's mediator — it was God's message — and yet he was also a representation of the people of Israel in that he was one of them.

The parallels with Jesus should be clear. He was one of us, fully human, and at the same time, chosen by God to be the mediator of his new covenant to humanity.

There's one other interesting use of the same word in the Greek (at least, the verb form of the word):

> *Because God wanted to make the unchanging nature of his purpose very clear to the heirs of what was promised, he confirmed it with an oath. (Heb 6:17)*

Did you spot it? It's the word 'confirmed,' surprisingly enough. Literally, God *mediated* his statement by an oath. Again, this is not a mediator in a legal dispute. Rather it is the mechanism by which the word comes to us, in this case, though an oath.

I know it's often hard to reprogram ourselves but we should try to catch ourselves every time we say the phrase: 'Jesus Christ, *our* mediator.' He is *God's* mediator, reaching out to me, reaching out to you, reaching out to all the world.

Summary

The Bible never describes Jesus as our *mediator, bringing our demands to God. Rather, it consistently describes him as the mediator of a new covenant, bringing the message from God to humanity. The direction is always: from God, to humanity.*

Discussion

1. What are the implications of thinking of Jesus as God's mediator rather than as our mediator?

2. Can you think of examples of biases in our translations? To what extent is it possible for translations to be free from bias?

Practical intercession

We have seen that Jesus is the mediator sent by God, and noted that the phrase "Jesus Christ *our* mediator" does not reflect Biblical usage. However, there is a pervasive idea in the New Testament of *intercession*. In particular, many passages talk of Jesus interceding for us.

Again, for many years, I had simply adopted a mainstream Christian view that intercession is Jesus pleading with God on my behalf. And yet, that view became challenged by so many passages, including by words of Jesus himself, that I felt the need to reexamine the basic doctrine, and see what the Biblical teaching is.

I'll jump to the punch line: once again I found that the traditional perspectives had done a 180 degree reversal of what the Bible was actually teaching. Whereas I had believed that Jesus was interceding with God on my behalf, instead I found the Bible teaching that he was interceding with me (or at least, in my life) on God's behalf.

That's quite a change of perspective!

The focus of intercession

Let's begin our reexamination in one of the classic intercession passages: Romans 8:34. We will take a block of verses leading up to it.

> *What, then, shall we say in response to this? If God is for us, who can be against us? he who did not spare his own Son, but gave him up for us all — how will he not also, along with him, graciously give us all things? Who will bring any charge against those whom God has chosen? It is God who justifies. Who is he that condemns? Christ Jesus, who died — more than that, who was raised to life — is at the right hand of God and is also interceding for us.*
> *(Rom 8:31-34)*

Before these verses, Paul has been emphasizing the role of spirit rather than law in the lives of believers, and then has been describing the grace of God in choosing, calling, justifying, and glorifying many sons and daughters in Christ. Very powerful and exciting stuff! And then come these verses as a reaction to his teaching about the abundant and all-sufficient grace of God. Let's reflect on the force of this passage.

First, Paul says, God is for us. That's foundational. God is on our side.

Second, if you want to know *how much* he is on our side, he has shown us by not sparing his son.

Third, if he didn't spare his own son, Paul says, can you imagine him not wanting to give us everything necessary to achieve salvation? Of course not!

So God is on our side, he's proved it by not sparing Jesus, and he intends to give us everything. But that's not all.

Fourth, in the light of this, who will bring any charge against us? Who will bring us to court? Paul is asking a rhetorical question. The implied answer is: No one! (If you are using the KJV, the words "*it is*" that the translators added here are really unhelpful to the flow: I think you should cross them out).

Who will bring any charge? No one! Because God is the one who justifies.

And fifth, "Who will condemn?" Again, the same answer is implied: No one! Why? Because the resurrected Jesus is at God's right hand.

So here's the argument Paul is making: God is on our side, he's proved it by not sparing Jesus, he intends to give us everything, he's the one who justifies us, and Jesus is at his right hand.

Then, having established that God is already on our side in every possible way, we read of Christ making intercession for us.

Can you make sense of that?

Given the context, it absolutely does not make sense to think of Christ's intercession as him pleading with God for us, as if he's our lawyer standing before the court of heaven. What would he be trying to do? To get God on our side? But God is already on our side! And he has proved it in every way possible leaving us with no conceivable doubt.

So it's worth asking, "Where is our problem in salvation?"

It is not with the Father. We don't need to change the Father's mind. There's never been a problem with the Father. The eternal spirit that fills the universe is exactly as he should be.

The real problem we face is in our battle against Sin.

Jesus intervenes and intercedes in our conflict with sin. He helps us through the difficult times of our lives, whether they are caused by internal temptations, or by external troubles and trials. And being at the right hand of God, with all authority in heaven and earth, he has access to all the resources of the universe.

Responding to our needs

If Jesus was expecting to be directly involved in our lives, we would imagine he would have told us. And indeed he did. Here's what he says in the middle of the *parakletos* (comforter) passage:

> *And I will do whatever you ask in my name, so that the Son may bring glory to the Father. You may ask me for anything in my name, and I will do it. (John 14:13-14)*

He makes it clear. He, Jesus, will act upon our prayers. If we know what we (or others) need, we just pray in Jesus' name, and he is the one who brings about the result.

However, this raises another possibility: what if we don't know what to pray for? Paul answers this, and his reply is directly in line with what we have been discovering.

> *In the same way, the Spirit helps us in our weakness. We do not know what we ought to pray for, but the Spirit himself intercedes for us with groans that words cannot express. And he who searches our hearts knows the mind of the Spirit, because [he]* intercedes for the saints in accordance with God's will. (Rom 8:26-27)*

This is another passage which has often been misunderstood. A popular interpretation is as follows: when we pray to God, we can't always express ourselves in a way that is appropriate; so the Holy Spirit takes those prayers, and refashions them with groans that words cannot

---

* *The NIV says "the Spirit" here, but the Greek is simply "he".*

express; this way, our prayer is presented acceptably to the Father on our behalf.

However, this interpretation raises all sorts of questions about the God whom we worship. Can he not hear faltering prayers, or is he confused by bad grammar? Is God not able to understand us, although he created us? Does the Spirit somehow have an ability that the Father doesn't, an ability to sort out the mess and straighten things up? It is very difficult to come up with any coherent understanding based on this interpretation.

Let's read the verses again, but with a different mindset. Instead of assuming that intercession is pleading with God, think of it as being an intervention in our lives. Now the verses are clear. Christ (in his spiritual presence) knows what we are going through. In our weakness there are times we really don't know what to pray for. Should we pray that someone we love be healed from their severe illness? Or should we pray that they may fall asleep and be released from pain? We face a quandary. But with the deepest empathy, Jesus intercedes in the situation. He becomes involved in ways words cannot express, his purpose being to accomplish the will of God, and bring us to the promised redemption. And so in all things he works for our good.

Incidentally, the word 'groaning' occurs earlier in this section:

> *We know that the whole creation has been groaning as in the pains of childbirth right up to the present time. Not only so, but we ourselves, who have the first-fruits of the Spirit, groan inwardly as we wait eagerly for our adoption as sons, the redemption of our [body]. (Rom 8:22-23)*

The whole creation is groaning and travailing in pain because of sin. Also, the sons of God groan inwardly, longing for the redemption of the whole body of Christ, waiting patiently in hope. Similarly, in the days of his flesh, Christ was moved with compassion, sighing and groaning within himself as he exerted himself to meet the needs of the people around him. He intervened in their lives and tackled their problems.

This passage tells us that nothing has changed. He is still doing it! Always. Even to the end of the age.

Interceding for Peter

To understand practical intercession better, let's see an example of Jesus' intercession at work.

Consider Peter's denial. As we trace through the circumstances around his denial, we will see a whole sequence of occasions in which Jesus interceded between Peter and his looming sin.

It starts when Jesus warns Peter that he was going to deny Jesus three times. Peter protests vehemently, "I won't deny you even though, every one else does." But Jesus starts his intercessory work: "You'll deny me three times, Peter."

See what's happening? Jesus is getting involved in the situation. He wants to rescue Peter from his sin, and failing that, to help him survive through it — even to come out the other side stronger for the experience. He's standing beside Peter. Jesus is the *parakletos,* there to assist him.

This is just the beginning. There are many other things that Jesus did to help Peter. First, his prayer:

> *Simon, Simon, Satan has asked to sift you as wheat. But I have prayed for you, Simon, that your faith may not fail. And when you have turned back, strengthen your brothers. (Luke 22:31-32)*

This request is particularly instructive. As we will see, Jesus is going to be personally involved in Peter's struggle, but there will also be a period of three days when he will be unable to help Peter. These next few hours and days will be crucial to Peter's eternal well-being, so Jesus is asking God to be directly involved. This powerful idea is very much present in Jesus' prayer heading up to Gethsemane.

> *I will remain in the world no longer, but they are still in the world, and I am coming to you. Holy Father, protect them by the power of your name – the name you gave me – so that they may be one as we are one. (John 17:11)*

Jesus knows that while he's dead, he will not be able to protect the disciples. He won't be on hand to intervene, and so he calls for the Father to carry on his protective and intercessory work.

Until that time comes, he's not finished. There are more things he can do to intercede for Peter.

In Gethsemane, Jesus exhorts Peter to keep awake, to pray and prepare.

> *"Why are you sleeping?" he asked them. "Get up and pray so that you will not fall into temptation." (Luke 22:46)*

"Prepare yourself, Peter," Jesus says. Preparation is essential if Peter is to resist the temptation coming his way.

Then there is a third intervention: after the three denials in the courtyard, as the cock crows, the Lord turned and looked at Peter (Luke 22:6). I can't imagine that there was condemnation in that look. Rather it was a look of compassion and concern. "I know you Peter, I know your heart. I love you Peter." Suddenly, caught short by the love of his Lord, Peter realizes what he has done! He goes out, and he weeps bitterly.

Because we know the story, we know that Peter's path of sin stops at this point. But how far might he have fallen without the intervention of Jesus? Would he have been maneuvered into calling for Jesus' crucifixion, or been required to curse him, or even been called upon to drive in the nails? And then what would his reaction have been? Fatal depression? Suicide?

We can't possibly know, but we do know that through this momentary intercession of Jesus, Peter takes the first step to recovery from the abyss of failure. He gets out of the situation he can't handle, and he weeps bitterly for the failure he has already exhibited.

The fourth: Jesus isn't finished. On the morning of the resurrection the angels instructed the women to give a special message of reassurance to Peter,

> *But go, tell his disciples and Peter, 'He is going ahead of you into Galilee. There you will see him, just as he told you.' (Mark 16:7)*

Fifth: he later made a special appearance to Peter. We don't have the details, but the visit was no doubt to give him further encouragement

> *They got up and returned at once to Jerusalem. There they found the Eleven and those with them, assembled together and saying, "It is true! The Lord has risen and has appeared to Simon."(Luke 24:33-34).*

And finally, on the shore of Galilee, Jesus gave Peter opportunity to match the three denials with a threefold declaration of his love and his loyalty. "Peter, do you love me?" "Lord, you know that I love you." And again. And again.

At least six separate acts of intercession!

This is what intercession is: the Lord intervening in the lives of his followers to help them in their struggle against weakness, temptation and sin. He does not put a hedge about them so that they never fall, but helps them through the experience, so that they come out stronger on the other side, so that they grow spiritually in preparation for the kingdom.

If the mortal Christ, in the midst of his arrest, trial, torture, crucifixion, and death, is able to intercede so effectively, how much more today: exalted to the right hand of God, enthroned in the heavens, with the powers of the universe his to command.

Now, isn't this exactly what we were reading earlier in 1 John 2:2? "My dear children, I write this to you so that you will not sin. But if anybody does sin we have a 'parakletos' with the Father." One who, by the will of the Father, stands beside us to comfort, strengthen and guide. Jesus Christ the righteous one.

Summary

Intercession happens when Jesus gets directly and personally involved in our lives, and helps us to overcome despite our weakness. This is seen in a practical example of Jesus interceding in the case of Peter.

Discussion

1. Before reading these last few sections, what ideas did you each have about *mediator*, *intercession,* and *comforter*? What do you think about them now?
2. Explore other occasions in which Jesus intervened in the lives of people to rescue them from sin? Was he successful? If so, why, and if not, why not?

cautions
prays for him
asks Peter to pray for himself
Sees Peter in his struggle
Reassures / Encourages
Restores him

Jesus as priest

Just as we often get the biblical concept of *mediator* the wrong way around, so I think we sometimes do with that of *priest*.

For a long time, I thought the purpose of a priest was to go to God and plead with him on behalf of the people. After all, the priest would take sacrifices, and would offer them. He would carry out all the necessary ritual under the law of Moses, presenting the sacrifice to God in the hope that God would see it, be pleased, and forgive the offerer.

It made sense to me, and I thought that the main purpose of a priest was to represent the people to God. But, you know what? I was looking at it backwards again!

On a closer examination, it becomes clear that, biblically, the main purpose of a priest is *not* to represent the people to God, rather it is to represent God to us. To see this, let's start by looking at sacrifices again.

It's not about sacrifices

Psalm 51 is stunning. It was written when David realized the terrible situation that he had got himself into — secretly sleeping with another man's wife, making her pregnant, trying to cover it up with deception, and finally resorting to murder.

Through the words of the prophet Nathan he has been confronted with his sin, and feels it deep within himself. While agonizing over how to be reconciled to God once again, he writes:

> *You do not delight in sacrifice, or I would bring it; you do not take pleasure in burnt offerings. The sacrifices of God are a broken spirit; a broken and contrite heart, O God, you will not despise. (Ps 51:16-17)*

Let's paraphrase this: "If you wanted dead animals, Lord, I would have brought them. But I know that's *not* what you really want. That's not what the Law is all about. What you really want is repentance and humility."

Certainly, the law required that the sacrifices be made, but only because of the effect they were designed to have on the people bringing the offerings. They were expected to learn from the process.

David recognizes this: "You don't want the sacrifice itself, Lord. What you want is a penitent spirit, a broken and a contrite heart."

Just pause for a moment, and be in awe of the immense spiritual insight of this man from 3000 years ago!

A little earlier, Samuel drives a similar point home to King Saul. Saul, in fear of a forthcoming battle, after waiting and waiting for Samuel, eventually decided to perform a sacrifice to get God on his side. Samuel then arrives and berates Saul for completely misunderstanding what sacrifice is all about.

> *But Samuel replied: "Does the LORD delight in burnt offerings and sacrifices as much as in obeying the voice of the LORD? To obey is better than sacrifice, and to heed is better than the fat of rams. (1 Sam 15:22)*

The sacrifice is not the point, Samuel says. Listening and responding to God is the point. It's not about the ritual, it's about the substance behind it.

> *To do what is right and just is more acceptable to the LORD than sacrifice. (Prov 21:3)*

Together, these passages tell us that if we see the primary work of a priest as presenting dead animals to God, we have missed the point.

So what is the primary work of the priest under the law?

Represent God to the people

Malachi gives us the lead we are looking for. In his second chapter, the prophet explains God's original covenant with the tribe of Levi, and what God expected of them if they are to continue in office. This is what he says:

> *True instruction was in his mouth and nothing false was found on his lips. He walked with me in peace and uprightness, and turned many from sin. For the lips of a priest ought to preserve knowledge, and from his mouth men should seek instruction — because he is the messenger of the LORD Almighty (Mal 2:6-7).*

Notice how this turns our earlier concept of a priest around? Previously, we described him as the *people's* representative going before God with their sacrifices.

But God says, "No! That's not what I intended in establishing the priesthood. The priest is to be *my* representative to the people. He should preserve knowledge, and provide instruction. He is *my* messenger. He should take *my* words and make them known to the people. He is to lead them away from sin. He must represent *me* to the people."

I find this an amazing verse — another one I had never noticed before. Of course, this is exactly the role that Christ exemplified during his ministry. He is God's priest, sent to turn many from sin. From his lips we seek instruction, because he is the messenger of the LORD Almighty.

It doesn't stop with Jesus. As his disciples, we are expected to carry out a similar role to others, so the same principle applies today. Consider Paul's exhortation that believers take the message of salvation to whoever will accept it:

> *All this is from God, who reconciled us to himself through Christ and gave us the ministry of reconciliation: that God was reconciling the world to himself in Christ, not counting men's sins against them. And he has committed to us the message of reconciliation. We are therefore Christ's ambassadors, as though God were making his appeal through us. We implore you on Christ's behalf: Be reconciled to God. (2 Cor 5:18-20)*

This is very like the Malachi passage; taking the message of reconciliation and salvation, and making it known to the people.

Notice that we are back to where we were earlier: the direction is from God to man. It begins with God, and he makes his appeal through Christ. The appeal is extended through the apostles appointed by Christ, and so on. All are representing God to the people. Not the other way round.

Made perfect

Even with this perspective, some passages about priests can still seem quite transactional, as if the priest is shifting something in heaven. Here's an example from Hebrews.

> *Day after day every priest stands and performs his religious duties; again and again he offers the same sacrifices, which can never take away sins. But when this priest had offered for all time one sacrifice for sins, he sat down at the right hand of God. Since that time he waits for his enemies to be made his footstool, because by one sacrifice he has made perfect forever those who are being made holy. (Heb 10:11-14)*

It's easy to read this passage as saying that while the animal sacrifices of the Law of Moses couldn't remove sin, the flawless sacrifice of Jesus was able to instantaneously make us blameless before God.

Again, I don't think we should read it that way. First, even in this verse, the writer implies a process: the sacrifice perfects those who are *being made* holy. That refers to a continuous process, not an instantaneous one.

Second, the writer immediately quotes a couple of passages from the Old Testament to clarify the point he is trying to make:

> *The Holy Spirit also testifies to us about this. First he says: "This is the covenant I will make with them after that time, says the Lord. I will put my laws in their hearts, and I will write them on their minds." Then he adds: "Their sins and lawless acts I will remember no more." And where these have been forgiven, there is no longer any sacrifice for sin. (Heb 10:15-18)*

Did you notice the two aspects that were chosen to emphasize? They are these: that God's ways will be deep in our hearts and minds; and that we will be forgiven. We can conclude that the sacrifice of Jesus has made us perfect by a process that works over time by transforming our hearts and minds to be in tune with God's ways, and that God willingly chooses to forgive us.

Our priest sacrificed himself as a witness from God to us, as an intervention in our lives.

Priestly intercession

Given that Jesus is a priest, he must be carrying out the fundamental priestly role that Malachi highlighted. He must still be representing God to his people, instructing us, guiding us, leading us away from sin. He is the messenger of the covenant.

Here's how it is described in Hebrews:

> *Now there have been many of those priests, since death prevented them from continuing in office; but because Jesus lives forever, he has a permanent priesthood. Therefore he is able to save completely those who come to God through him, because he always lives to intercede for them. (Heb 7:23-25)*

Jesus, we are told, has a permanent priesthood; he is a priest for ever. One who can save completely.

The writer connects the idea of Jesus "saving completely" with the fact that he lives forever. I think the idea is this: Jesus gets to know us through our lives, our strengths and weaknesses, our trigger points. Because he knows us so well, he can be truly effective. Every day, he carries out his priestly work of getting involved in the lives of those for whom he is appointed. If his priesthood were temporary, he would need to be replaced by another who has not come to know us, and so would be less effective.

Jesus is effective because he *always lives* to intercede for us. But then there's that idea of 'intercession' again.

As we have seen, we should not think, "Ah, yes, that means intercede *with God* for them." It doesn't say that. Let's be really clear. It does *not* say that he is interceding *with God.* It simply says he is going to intercede for believers. We have already seen what that means.

Just to drive the point home, let's ask the question: where do we need intercession? Who or what is it that we have a problem with? Do we have a problem with God. Or do we have a problem with Sin?

The answer is clear. We don't have a problem with God at all. It isn't God who needs to change his ways.

But if Jesus is interceding *in our lives* in the battle against Sin, in the very area where we *do* need to change, then suddenly his priestly role makes sense. Here is a priest who gets involved day by day in the lives of those who are coming to God through him.

To expand on the earlier analogy of being stuck in a pit: Jesus doesn't save us by convincing the (heavenly) authorities to come looking for us. Rather he comes himself and lifts us out, with all the power and capabilities of the authorities themselves.

He is the messenger of the covenant. He is here with us as God's representative for our benefit: to save us from the destructiveness of sin. He is able to save us "completely".

Summary

As priest, Jesus' main role is to be in our lives, to instruct us, to represent God's way to us, and to rescue us from the destructiveness of sin.

Discussion

1. Think of some priests in the Bible. Does their work seem to be described well by Malachi 2:7?
2. During his ministry, Jesus was representing God to humanity. What is he doing now? Discuss if you have had an experience that may have been Jesus interceding in your life.

Book of life

Jesus my savior, my priest. Also, Jesus my judge. Born a human child, he grew both physically and spiritually, until he was perfected by the nurturing and discipline of his Father, in which he was a full participant. Now he is glorified, elevated to the right-hand of God, and entrusted with all authority in heaven and earth.

What an accomplishment! What a mighty work the Father has wrought. God manifested in the flesh!

When Jesus' victory over sin was complete, he ascended to heaven and sat at the right hand of God. Here's how the author of Hebrews describes that moment:

> *When Christ came as high priest of the good things that are already here, he went through the greater and more perfect tabernacle that is not man-made, that is to say, not a part of this creation. He did not enter by means of the blood of goats and calves; but he entered the Most Holy Place once for all by his own blood, having obtained eternal redemption. (Heb 9:11-12)*

These are powerful words: Jesus entering the temple of heaven, with his blood as an offering.

I think that we have a more detailed account of this event within our Bibles. It may not be obvious at first, but I am convinced that this is what the apostle John sees worked out in the early part of his revelation.

The Throne Room

In Revelation 4, John experiences being drawn up to heaven; to the tabernacle of heaven. If you don't recall the section well enough, it would be worth pausing to read it, to set the scene in your mind; but let me summarize it anyway.

John sees the cherubim, the chariots of God, surrounding the throne, bright and fiery. The throne itself is filled with the glory of God, so bright that John can barely see any details. The whole atmosphere is resplendent with mightiness and majesty. There is a sea of glass before the throne, like the huge wash bowl of the tabernacle, and golden bowls and incense are in the hands of those around the throne.

Praise and glory is being offered to God, both for who he is, and for what he has done.

In this context, Revelation 5 picks up the narrative:

> *Then I saw in the right hand of him who sat on the throne a scroll with writing on both sides and sealed with seven seals. And I saw a mighty angel proclaiming in a loud voice, "Who is worthy to break the seals and open the scroll?" But no one in heaven or on earth or under the earth could open the scroll or even look inside it. I wept and wept because no one was found who was worthy to open the scroll or look inside. (Rev 5:1-4)*

Later we discover that the scroll — the book — in God's right hand is the Book of Life. John knows what it is, and to his horror he sees that the book is closed! Shut tight, and sealed! There is no one worthy to open the scroll, no one worthy to open the Book of Life. No one is able to act as savior and judge to humanity on God's behalf.

What a terrible truth!

The blackness of despair overwhelms John, and he weeps and weeps. Centuries of grief well up in him, and he wails for lost humanity. All this glory around him, and humanity is estranged and lost! This is hopelessness, going down into the pit with no one to rescue. John is devastated. His grief is for himself, and for us, and for everyone who has ever lived. He experiences the wretchedness and desperation of our situation, and he is overwhelmed. Here is the Book of Life in the hand of the Almighty, and it is sealed!

In the midst of his sorrow, one of the elders comforts him.

> *"Do not weep! See, the Lion of the tribe of Judah, the Root of David, has triumphed. He is able to open the scroll and its seven seals." (Rev 5:5)*

You can imagine John's emotions at this point. Hope beyond hope! Anticipation!

He turns around, looking for this mighty lion… And he sees a lamb! A lamb standing before the throne, looking like it has been slain.

Here is Jesus!

Here is Jesus in the most significant event in the history of heaven and earth. Here he is, presenting his blood to his Father as a mark of accomplishment, as a mark of what he has achieved in his Father's name.

"I have overcome," the blood whispers. "Not my will, but yours be done," it declares. I can imagine that heaven is hushed at this moment. Hushed with awe, and wonder at this man who says with simple and absolute truth, "I desire to do your will, O Lord."

He came and took the scroll from the right hand of him who sat on the throne. When he had taken it, the four living creatures and the twenty-four elders fell down to worship the Lamb. They sang a new song:

> *You are worthy to take the scroll and to open its seals, because you were slain, and with your blood you purchased men for God from every tribe and language and people and nation. You have made them to be a kingdom and priests to serve our God, and they will reign on the earth. (Rev 5:9-10)*

O the wonder of it! He is worthy to open the book! Lord Jesus Messiah!

Paying the Price

His victory was very costly. The elders and living creatures are driven to praise because the lamb was slain, and because he 'purchased' or 'redeemed' (KJV) us for God. If we're not careful, that word 'purchased' could sound very transactional, even like the older notion that God paid the devil for our salvation! I don't think we should think of it that way at all, of course. So what does 'purchased' mean?

In their Greek dictionary, Louw and Nida[*] describe the meaning of the Greek word here as, *to cause the release or freedom of someone by a means which proves costly to the individual causing the release.* In other words, the notion of 'purchased' here doesn't imply 'purchased from someone else', but rather, 'paid the price for'. Jesus purchased us for God in that he paid the price for us.

That might not seem like much of a difference, but think of it this way. Suppose I told you that I ran the marathon yesterday and now I'm paying the price for it. I would not mean that I'm still trying to get the entrance fee together! It's not about money — I wouldn't be thinking about payment at all. Rather, I would be referring to the toll it took on me. I would mean that I feel the consequences of the effort in my muscles and ligaments and bones.

So it is with Christ. In his flesh, he bore the consequences both of drawing us to the Father, and also of the personal discipline he underwent to mold his will to God's. It came at a huge personal cost, and it was a cost he had to bear, but he's not buying something from someone else. You see the distinction?

The purchase metaphor is attractive — we were bought from our old master — but if we're not careful it can easily run out of control. As in most cases, metaphors have a certain application, and then should be carefully laid aside, otherwise we find ourselves with a load of confusion. In this case, the plain fact is that our salvation cost Jesus his life. That was the price, the toll it took. It's just like the parable of the good shepherd. The shepherd died in the battle with the wolf. The flock was safe, but at the cost of their shepherd's life. He bore the cost of the sheep's safety.

In passing, just pause for a moment and note a beautiful metaphorical twist here in the revelation: the shepherd himself is a lamb...

The lamb goes forward, and takes the book from his Father's hand. In the Revelation narrative, this is now his book, referred to later as *the Lamb's book of life* (Rev 21:27)

---

[*] *Louw & Nida, Greek-English Lexicon of the New Testament: Based on Semantic Domains, United Bible Societies, 1988.*

Because of the lamb, life and salvation is now possible. Finally, there is a savior judge who is able, who is worthy, to bring about the fulfillment of all that God has been promising. The promises can be fulfilled, and the book can now be unsealed, seal by seal as history unfolds, until it will finally be open!

A Scriptural Theme

This is not the first time the idea of the book of life occurs in Scripture. In fact, the book of life theme runs through both the old and new testaments.

In Malachi, we read:

> *Then those who feared the LORD talked with each other, and the LORD listened and heard. A scroll of remembrance was written in his presence concerning those who feared the LORD and honored his name. "They will be mine," says the LORD Almighty, "in the day when I make up my treasured possession. I will spare them, just as in compassion a man spares his son who serves him. And you will again see the distinction between the righteous and the wicked, between those who serve God and those who do not. (Mal 3:16-18)*

It doesn't say 'Book of Life' here, but it's still pretty clear that is what's being described. The scroll of remembrance is going to be used to identify who belongs to God. These are the ones he will remember in that day, in the day he makes up his treasured possession.

Daniel is more explicit:

> *At that time Michael, the great prince who protects your people, will arise. There will be a time of distress such as has not happened from the beginning of nations until then. But at that time your people – everyone whose name is found written in the book – will be delivered. Multitudes who sleep in the dust of the earth will awake: some to everlasting life, others to shame and everlasting contempt. (Dan 12:1-2)*

The context is really clear. This is resurrection and judgment. The book is used to determine who will be delivered from the judgments God brings upon humanity.

A thousand years earlier, Moses also understood this very well. After the incident of the golden calf, Moses said to God,

> *Oh, what a great sin these people have committed! They have made themselves gods of gold. But now, please forgive their sin – but if not, then blot me out of the book you have written. (Ex 32:32)*

I'm not quite sure what Moses' motivation is here. It could read like emotional blackmail: either (a) forgive the people or (b) condemn them and reject me too. If so, he's trying to twist God's arm and force God to forgive all the Israelites by putting his own salvation on the line.

However, given the depth of Moses' humility, I think we should seek a better explanation. I think it is more likely that Moses feels personally responsible for the idolatry of the people. He recognizes that the people have failed, and believes that as their leader he bears equal responsibility for their failure, and so should share in their punishment, even eternal condemnation.

God's response is firm. He says,

> *Whoever has sinned against me I will blot out of my book. Now go, lead the people to the place I spoke of, and my angel will go before you. However, when the time comes for me to punish, I will punish them for their sin (Ex 32:33,34).*

Leaving aside Moses' intent, there is a vital inference we can draw from this interchange. Ask yourself, when is the book of life written? We each hope and expect that our name will be in the book in that day, but *when* will our names be entered in it?

Think of this: Moses said, "Blot my name out of the book." This only makes sense if he has confidence that his name is already in the book. It couldn't have been blotted out if it wasn't written in already. So we conclude: the book of life is being written now! Our names are entered during our lives.

Written today!

We can draw the same conclusion from Malachi's day. A scroll of remembrance was written then, while the people were meeting together.

This picture is repeated again and again and again. The book of life is being written now. It's not going to be written at the resurrection — it's being written now.

Consider the following passage in Hebrews, which contains yet more evidence of this. The writer is drawing a contrast between Zion and Sinai.

> *You have not come to a mountain that can be touched and that is burning with fire; to darkness, gloom and storm; to a trumpet blast or to such a voice speaking words that those who heard it begged that no further word be spoken to them, because they could not bear what was commanded: "If even an animal touches the mountain, it must be stoned." The sight was so terrifying that Moses said, "I am trembling with fear."*
>
> *But you have come to Mount Zion, to the heavenly Jerusalem, the city of the living God. You have come to thousands upon thousands of angels in joyful assembly, to the church of the firstborn, whose names are written in heaven. You have come to God, the judge of all men, to the spirits of righteous men made perfect, to Jesus the mediator of a new covenant, and to the sprinkled blood that speaks a better word than the blood of Abel. (Heb 12:18-24)*

Notice that it is not those whose names *will be* written in heaven. The church of the firstborn is made up of those whose names are *already* written in heaven.

Today, your name is (or is not) in the book of life.

> *He has set his foundation on the holy mountain; the LORD loves the gates of Zion more than all the dwellings of Jacob. Glorious things are said of you, O city of God: "I will record Rahab and Babylon among those who acknowledge me – Philistia too, and Tyre, along with Cush – and will say, 'This one was born in Zion.'" Indeed, of Zion it will be said, "This one and that one were born in her, and the Most High himself will establish her." The LORD will write in the register of the peoples: "This one was born in Zion." (Ps 87:1-6)*

Where is your birthplace? Your spiritual birthplace I mean.

It's written, "This one was born in Zion." It's in the register of the peoples, "This one, and this one and this and this... this one was born in Zion." What a wonderful picture! In a sense I wasn't born in England; you weren't born in the United States, or Australia, or Asia, or wherever. Not really. Sure, yes, you were — physically.

But when you underwent baptism you were declaring, "I'm going to be born again; I'm being born in Zion." Your name was written in the register of the peoples, "This one was born in Zion." A very powerful scripture.

Summary

John has a vision of the tabernacle in heaven in which Jesus, the Lamb, presents his blood as a mark of his submission and commitment. In acknowledgment of his accomplishment, and the awful price he paid, he is given the right to open the Book of Life. This Book records the names of those who are being saved. It is being written now.

Discussion

1. What is the relationship between the book of life, and forgiveness?
2. Do you think your name is in the book of life? Are you sure you would like it to be? How does this show up in your life choices?
3. Read some other passages which look at the throne of God in heaven (e.g. Ex 24:9-11, Is 6:1-4, Ezek 1:22-28), and compare with this passage in Revelation.

Confidence in the judgment

When Christ returns to set up God's kingdom here on earth, one of the first things he does is raise the dead, and make his judgment about each one. This is how Jesus himself expresses it:

> *"Do not be amazed at this, for a time is coming when all who are in their graves will hear his voice and come out – those who have done good will rise to live, and those who have done evil will rise to be condemned. By myself I can do nothing; I judge only as I hear, and my judgment is just, for I seek not to please myself but him who sent me." (John 5:28-30)*

Paul describes it similarly to the Christians in Corinth:

> *For we must all appear before the judgment seat of Christ, that each one may receive what is due him for the things done while in the body, whether good or bad. (2 Cor 5:10)*

This idea is not new to either Jesus or Paul. The Old Testament prophets had already described the judgment in some detail. Daniel, for example, was given a vision which he retells as follows:

> *As I looked, thrones were set in place, and the Ancient of Days took his seat. His clothing was as white as snow; the hair of his head was white like wool. His throne was flaming with fire, and its wheels were all ablaze. A river of fire was flowing, coming out from before him. Thousands upon thousands attended him; ten thousand times ten thousand stood before him. The court was seated, and the books were opened…*
>
> *In my vision at night I looked, and there before me was one like a son of man, coming with the clouds of heaven. He approached the Ancient of Days and was led into his presence. He was given authority, glory and sovereign power; all peoples, nations and men*

> *of every language worshiped him. His dominion is an everlasting dominion that will not pass away, and his kingdom is one that will never be destroyed. (Dan 7:9-14)*

The impressive majesty and stature of the scene comes through loud and clear, as does the prominent role of one who can only be Jesus. There are also many of the same elements as were described in John's later vision in the Revelation 4-5 passage we considered in the previous section, because they are set in the same backdrop of God's throne room.

Daniel's vision mentions 'the books' being opened. These books were presumably record books that the kings would maintain to know how to govern. There's an example of this in Esther when King Xerxes reviews the events of his empire.

> *That night the king could not sleep; so he ordered the book of the chronicles, the record of his reign, to be brought in and read to him. (Esth 6:1)*

Similarly, towards the end of the book of Revelation, when John relates his equivalent to Daniel's vision, we again find this element of "the books".

> *Then I saw a great white throne and him who was seated on it. Earth and sky fled from his presence, and there was no place for them. And I saw the dead, great and small, standing before the throne, and books were opened. Another book was opened, which is the book of life. The dead were judged according to what they had done as recorded in the books. The sea gave up the dead that were in it, and death and Hades gave up the dead that were in them, and each person was judged according to what he had done. Then death and Hades were thrown into the lake of fire. The lake of fire is the second death. If anyone's name was not found written in the book of life, he was thrown into the lake of fire. (Rev 20:11-15)*

The books are the records of everything that has ever happened. I don't think these have to be literal books. If we were writing the account nowadays we would say, 'and the database was accessed' or something like that. The important fact is that there are records of everything that had been done. And along with the records, there is another book, the book of life.

How do these books relate to each other?

It seems to me that "the books" contain plenty of evidence to condemn us all! All the acts of love and hate, of peace and war, of generosity and selfishness are recorded here. If these books are the sole authority, not one of us would be saved. If salvation depended on our works, on our ability to do right and never wrong, then we would all be lost.

But these books are not the sole authority! The book of life is also present! And it is open!!

If your name is in the book of life, the other books are irrelevant. They contain events and circumstances that have been forgiven. Your name is in the book! You are welcomed with open arms! With the joy of thousands upon thousands of angels, and with the love and delight of your Lord who thought your life was worth everything he was ever able to give.

> *He who overcomes will, like them, be dressed in white. I will never blot out his name from the book of life, but will acknowledge his name before my Father and his angels. He who has an ear, let him hear what the Spirit says to the churches. (Rev 3:5-6)*

It's a wonderful promise!

Confidence

But do I expect to be there? Do you? Do you expect to be welcomed into eternity, or are you worried that you may be shut out?

It's easy to lack courage and confidence in our salvation. "I'm not good enough," we think. "I have sins and faults." How can we build personal confidence? How can we realize that this is not all theoretical, but it is about me and you? Will *I* be there?

There's a hint of a situation in the church at Philippi which I take as a personal exhortation. Here's what Paul says in his letter to them:

> *I plead with Euodia and I plead with Syntyche to agree with each other in the Lord. Yes, and I ask you, loyal yokefellow, help these women who have contended at my side in the cause of the gospel, along with Clement and the rest of my fellow workers, whose names are in the book of life. (Phil 4:2-3)*

Two thousand years later it's hard to know exactly what was going on, but there seems to be bickering in the church. Maybe even strong disagreements. Euodia and Syntyche don't get along with each other. Not like today, right?!

The situation is sufficiently tense that they need some help to sort it out, so they can be supportive of each other. But here's the wonderful thing: even in the middle of their challenging interpersonal situation, their names are still in the book of life!

That, to me, is a great reassurance!

The Lord knows our failings; he knows our frailty; he knows our limitations. He's not surprised when he looks in your heart and sees sin, and sees temptation — he knows it's there!

The Father, in his love, reaches out to us. He has designed his plan of salvation to take account of this. He trained his son to be able to strengthen us in our weakness, to help us with our limitations, to encourage us to yearn for something better and more fulfilling. And so, despite our failings, our names are entered into the book of life.

Moreover, the fact that it is being written now is a great reassuring principle to bear in mind. Are you in covenant with Christ? Is he truly your lord? Does he express the deepest desires of your heart? If you can answer yes to these, then be confident! Your name is already written in heaven. Already you have moved from Death to Life.

Perfect love

Here's a final thought. While I have confidence in the judgment, I cannot know for sure. Paul even urges us to show caution:

> *Therefore judge nothing before the appointed time; wait till the Lord comes. He will bring to light what is hidden in darkness and will expose the motives of men's hearts. At that time each will receive his praise from God. (1 Cor 4:5)*

What then? Do I live in fear of the judgment, with no idea how it will turn out?

Of course not! Insofar as I truly know myself, I know that I desire the things of God. I desire to be one with him, to be one with Christ, to be one with all other disciples. Moreover, I know with certainty that he is willing and able to forgive me, to take my sins away and count me righteous if that is truly what I want; if that expresses the deepest desire of my heart.

But what about the risk that I have been deceiving myself all these years, and that I discover I don't want the things of God and of right ways? What then?

Even in that case I can have true confidence.

What I mean is this. I have confidence that when I come to the judgment seat — it's impossible for me to write this without emotion — and my judge looks me in the eye... If at that moment he says, "You never really wanted this, did you?" I will know that he knows who I am...

Here is an exquisite man, a man who loves me beyond words. Here is a man who knows me more deeply and intimately than I know myself. Here is a man who can truly assess whether the Father's kingdom would be delight or torment for me. From that man, I can accept his judgment whatever it is...

> *... Whoever lives in love lives in God, and God in him. In this way, love is made complete among us so that we will have confidence on the day of judgment, because in this world we are like him. There is no fear in love. But perfect love drives out fear, because fear has to do with punishment. The one who fears is not made perfect in love. (1 John 4:16-18)*

That is my confidence. He loves me more than I love myself, more deeply and more meaningfully.

If I can stand in confidence even in the smallest possibility of rejection, how much more in the abundant expectation of acceptance!

Summary

Our relationship with Christ gives us confidence that our names are written in the Book of Life, despite our weaknesses and imperfections. The completeness of his love for us gives us overwhelming confidence about his judgment towards us.

Discussion

1. To what extent do you have confidence in the love and compassion of Jesus towards you?

2. How strong is your personal relationship with Jesus? What effect does that have on your readiness to face him in judgment?

Afterword

If the Bible tries very hard to explain why Jesus died, then why is it so hard to find a compelling explanation?

I think the main problem is that we don't have the luxury of coming to the Bible without preconceived notions and ideas. We come with ideas that have been picked up from popular culture, and these ideas muddy the waters. They affect even the way we understand words themselves.

Consider this example: Suppose I say that *I believe in God.* What does it mean? Well, we all know what it means. It means I have an intellectual acceptance of the existence of God, that God is there — that God is a real being. Right?

Okay, but now let's take a second example. Suppose I say that *I believe in the President.* What does that mean? Astonishingly, it means something *completely different!* This time it's not about an intellectual assent that the man exists. It's much more about trust, about whether I trust this man to do things that are good for the nation.

You see the distinction? The words: 'believe in' — God or the President — are exactly the same for each statement, but we lay on top of them a particular understanding that comes from our preconceptions about how words are used.

In day-to-day speaking we share enough of a common context with the speaker. We can get by with understanding what each other is saying — more or less, anyway. But problems can easily arise when we read the Bible because contextual understanding has shifted significantly over the 2,000 years since the New Testament was written. We can end up reading things into the text that might astonish the original authors!

Metaphors and Symbols

The span of time is particularly challenging when Biblical authors used allegories and metaphors. When allegories or parables are understood *metaphorically*, they can be very helpful. When, however, they are taken as literal, they can become problematic.

To see an example, consider the parable of the rich man and Lazarus (Luke 16:19-31). In the parable, Abraham gets to talk to the rich man after they have both died, but is unable to do anything to alleviate the rich man's suffering. I have met Christians who take this to be a literal description of life after death. But this would mean that the redeemed will always have to observe and interact with those suffering eternal torment! Surely Jesus didn't mean us to reach this conclusion, especially as it would contradict many other passages about peace and contentment in the time to come (e.g. Rev 21:4).

In contrast, if the parable is understood purely as a parable, then the problematic implications disappear. Parables or allegories are stories designed to make a point, to convey a specific teaching. In this case, Jesus makes very clear what the lesson of the story is (Luke 16:31). The point of the parable was simply that even the resurrection would not be sufficient to convince those who choose not to believe. It's the punch line of the whole story. If the parable is taken as a fictional story intended to drive this point home, then it is very powerful. If it's taken further, as a literal description of the afterlife, then it becomes problematic.

I don't want to leave an impression that metaphors and symbols are not useful or important. Not at all! They have great value when understood for what they are: symbols, allegories, metaphors, and so on. After all, Jesus used allegories — parables — extensively in his teaching.

It is only when we understand the underlying teaching that we can also fully understand the allegories, as the disciples found out when they had to ask Jesus to explain what his parables meant, and on multiple occasions!

The same occurs with the death of Jesus. When the metaphors and symbols used about his death are taken as literal statements, we can end up in complex and technical discussions about exactly what transaction was taking place when Jesus died; and these conclusions are often at odds with plain teachings elsewhere in the Bible. Instead, if we notice that a statement about Jesus' death may be allegorical, then we have the opportunity to ask what the metaphor or symbol is trying to say, and so learn a lesson that is directly relevant to how we live our lives today.

Of course, both the time-challenge and the allegory-challenge imply a need for interpretation, and interpretation is notoriously subject to bias.

I can't be sure that something like that hasn't happened in this study, even though I have diligently tried not to bring my own *a priori* thinking. It is almost impossible to avoid. Thus, as I suggested in the introduction, please treat these thoughts as meditations on the topic. Through them, I hope the words of scripture have been able to reach out to each one of us.

There is also much left unexplored. Though we have touched on a few of them, understanding all the various Biblical metaphors and symbols is too large a task for us here. That will have to remain as (a lifetime's worth of) homework for each of us!

Summary

Through this study we covered so much ground that it's possible to have lost sight of the big picture. Why did Jesus die? I believe there are two reasons given in the Bible.

First, he died as a witness to us.

His death showed us the utter sinfulness of sin in a way that we cannot argue away — his death was a clarion call to wake us up as we watch in horror the violence that people like us did to him. When we really appreciate the murder of Christ, we realize that sin isn't something little. It's not just a case of, "Oh well, I'll try to be a little bit better than I used to be…" His death challenges us to pick one side or another. In the face of his death, we can't sit on the fence. We must choose.

Do I want destructiveness, or do I want life?

His death transforms our shades of grey into a black and white starkness that is shocking.

At the same time, his death was a witness of the love he and his Father have for us. Can we be in any doubt of the lengths God will go to save us? Do we have any reason at all to be cautious about trusting in Jesus' desire for each of us to share eternity with him?

> *Greater love has no one than this, that he lay down his life for his friends. (John 15:13)*

He died to inspire us, to encourage us to be different, and to show us the path in which we need to walk.

> *For Christ's love compels us, because we are convinced that one died for all, and therefore all died. And he died for all, that those who live should no longer live for themselves but for him who died for them and was raised again. (2 Cor 5:14-15)*

And he died as a witness that wherever we are in this life, and whatever darkness surrounds us, he has been there too. He understands. And he will draw us through it if we let him.

All of this is his witness to us.

And second, he died to give up his flesh.

In his own personal discipleship, he learned obedience to God. He fought against temptations. He rejected this life. In every way possible he gave up his life. And so he found it (Matt 16:25).

He died as a final act of giving up his flesh. Flesh or spirit? He chose spirit.

And God saved him! Saved him from death, and elevated him to the highest place. He is seated at the right hand of God, and granted authority to save and judge. The way to fulfillment of the promises of God was now open!

Now, we have a resurrected Lord who is overseeing and guiding our own paths of discipleship. He is teaching and training us, encouraging us to submit to his discipleship, and intervening in our lives at the point of conflict with sin. He is our savior, day by day.

He is our savior, and he is our judge. He has authority to raise us from the dead, and declare that we are his. He has authority to forgive us, and to declare us clean. He has authority to welcome us to share eternity in glorious harmony, united with God who fills all time and space, and united with each other.

Conclusion

Taken together, I believe that these two reasons summarize the wealth of Biblical teaching on the subject. Strip away the metaphor, look behind the allegory, and in each case I think you will find one of the reasons above. No transaction in heaven. No human blood sacrifice, but a witness to us, and a total submission to God rather than flesh.

We need to be changed, not only by his death, but also by his life. While we participate in the transformational training of Christ, God relinquishes all right to bring retribution to us. He is at peace with our intent.

We live the forgiven life.

We can give great and abundant thanks that God has appointed Jesus to be an active high priest, that he is always there to intervene, to help guide, strengthen, and comfort us day by day, in preparation for his coming in glory.

> *'On that day you will realize that I am in my Father, and you are in me, and I am in you. Whoever has my commands and obeys them, he is the one who loves me.*
>
> *He who loves me will be loved by my Father, and I too will love him and show myself to him.' Then Judas (not Judas Iscariot) said, 'But, Lord, why do you intend to show yourself to us and not to the world?'*
>
> *Jesus replied, 'If anyone loves me, he will obey my teaching. My Father will love him, and we will come to him and make our home with him. (John 14:20-23)*

Through his transforming work in each one of us, our righteous responses become part of our character rather than a duty we have to fulfill. This is salvation: intervention to the extent that it becomes permanent, because a unity of thought, purpose and action has developed between savior and saint. Christ is formed within us! (Gal 4:19)

We pray, that through the work of our savior judge, we may fully participate in this incredibly great honor.

May God be praised.

Index of Quotations

Gen 1; 128, 137
Gen 2; 8
Gen 3; 56
Gen 9; 47
Gen 22; 28
Gen 44; 9
Gen 45; 25
Ex 7; 126
Ex 24; 65, 171
Ex 32; 169
Ex 34; 75
Lev 16; 26
Deut 12; 46
Deut 18; 100-101, 128
1 Sam 8; 134
1 Sam 15; 159
2 Kings 15; 134
Esth 6; 173
Job 1; 91
Job 40; 91
Ps 33; 128
Ps 40; 84
Ps 49; 7
Ps 50; 66
Ps 51; 67, 85, 158
Ps 87; 170
Ps 91; 114
Ps 106; 109
Ps 145; 142
Prov 16; 80
Prov 17; 11
Prov 21; 159
Is 5; 11
Is 6; 58-59, 90, 171
Is 40; 126
Is 43; 99
Is 46; 64
Is 53; 23, 26-27, 107
Is 55; 126, 129
Is 59; 99, 107
Jer 7; 106
Jer 17; 124
Ezek 1; 95, 171
Ezek 18; 12
Ezek 22; 106
Dan 7; 173
Dan 12; 13, 168
Mic 6; 67, 85
Hab 1; 62
Mal 2; 160
Mal 3; 79, 168

Matt 1; 128
Matt 4; 112
Matt 9; 136
Matt 10; 47
Matt 14; 116, 122
Matt 16; 19, 181
Matt 20; 6
Matt 22; 82
Matt 26; 32, 40, 119-120
Matt 28; 141
Mark 10; 42
Mark 16; 156
Luke 1; 58
Luke 4; 111
Luke 5; 141
Luke 8; 41
Luke 9; 42, 47
Luke 12; 119
Luke 13; 108
Luke 15; 15
Luke 16; 179
Luke 18; 51, 61
Luke 20; 104
Luke 22; 155-156
Luke 23; 24, 30
Luke 24; 156
John 1; 129
John 3; 28, 136
John 5; 91, 132, 172
John 6; 38, 117
John 8; 42
John 10; 39, 66
John 13; 126
John 14; 18, 36, 91, 128, 142, 146, 153, 182
John 15; 180
John 16; 140
John 17; 64, 155
John 19; 30
Acts 2; 24
Acts 3; 33, 102
Acts 5; 135
Acts 7; 24, 141
Acts 17; 36, 132
Rom 3; 52, 70, 85
Rom 4; 33, 70-71
Rom 5; 93-95
Rom 6; 8, 14, 37
Rom 7; 31, 92
Rom 8; 151, 153-154
Rom 12; 87
Rom 14; 83
1 Cor 4; 175
1 Cor 15; 1, 33
2 Cor 3; 137
2 Cor 5; 93, 160, 172, 181
2 Cor 12; 26
Eph 1; 64
Eph 2; 90
Eph 5; 29
Gal 3; 149
Gal 4; 92, 182
Col 1; 18, 130, 135
Col 2; 64
Col 3; 137
Phil 2; 66, 96, 125, 127

Phil 3; 19, 122
Phil 4; 174
1 Thess 4; 124
1 Tim 1; 99
1 Tim 2; 147
2 Tim 1; 64
Titus 1; 99
Titus 3; 35
Heb 1; 91, 130
Heb 2; 39, 51, 102, 110, 124
Heb 3; 102
Heb 4; 61, 100, 103, 130
Heb 5; 111, 121, 123
Heb 6; 149
Heb 7; 140, 162
Heb 8; 65
Heb 9; 45, 48, 53, 66, 148, 164
Heb 10; 60, 93, 161
Heb 11; 72
Heb 12; 148, 170
Jas 2; 71
Jas 4; 84
1 Pet 1; 137
1 Pet 2; 19
1 Pet 3; 1, 34
1 John 1; 13
1 John 2; 49, 53, 125, 145-146, 157
1 John 3; 125
1 John 4; 53, 82, 96, 176
Rev 3; 62, 174
Rev 5; 165-166
Rev 13; 64
Rev 19; 130
Rev 20; 173
Rev 21; 167, 179

Subject Index

A

Abelard, 14

Abraham, 28, 42, 70-71, 102, 104, 127, 133, 179

Adam and Eve, 56, 60, 64

allegory, 9, 179, 181

angry, 25, 49, 89, 93, 142

Anselm, 7

Aquinas, 7

arm of the Lord, 106

ashamed, 57, 94

atonement, 2, 6, 44, 49, 72

authority, 66, 136, 141, 172

B

baptism, 34, 36, 96, 111, 119, 121, 170

Barnabas, 72

believe, 1, 28, 37, 60, 70-71, 73, 93, 107, 140-141, 178

betray, 23-24, 32

Bible, 2-3, 11, 17, 20, 44, 46, 49, 56, 98, 129, 145, 178

blame, 13, 94, 98

blasphemy, 140

blood, 23, 44-48, 52, 55-56, 66, 84-85, 102, 130, 166, 181

Book of Life, 165, 167-171, 173-176

breach, 106, 108-109

C

commands, 83, 125, 182

compassion, 41, 79, 85, 154

confidence, 60, 100, 174

conscience, 34, 48, 93, 148

constraint, 75, 132

covenant, 45, 146, 175

covering, 55

crucifixion, 24

cup, 119

D

Daniel, 101

David, 71, 85, 105, 134

death, 8, 12, 25, 41, 122, 126-127, 133, 137, 162, 173, 180

death of Jesus, 2, 5-6, 16, 20-21, 29, 33-34, 179

devil, 6, 39, 112, 120

Diaglott, 52-53

dispensations, 69, 72

divine nature, 135, 137

doctrine of salvation, 1

dread, 58, 101

E

Ezekiel, 95, 105

F

faith, 18, 33, 41, 52, 61, 70-73, 83-84, 90, 93-94, 98, 102, 127, 155

Father, 38, 123, 140, 153

Father's will, 111, 119, 127, 142-143

fear, 39, 57-58, 60, 80, 95-96, 101, 133, 170, 175-176

fig tree, 108

five thousand, 116

flesh, 39, 85, 92, 94, 102, 110, 113, 119, 121, 124, 128-129, 135, 167, 181

forgive, 20, 74, 90, 92, 140-141, 175

forgiveness, 12, 33-34, 44, 98, 139

freewill, 76, 84

G

gave his life, 38, 98

Gethsemane, 18, 23, 40, 85, 118, 140, 155

glory of God, 58, 70, 74, 165

God's will, 23, 26, 124, 137, 153

Golgotha, 2, 19, 27, 29, 36, 38, 40, 42, 47, 99, 120, 123

good shepherd, 38, 167

grace, 14, 21, 25, 35, 61, 64, 70, 94, 136, 152

Greek, 3, 49-50, 52-53, 73, 99, 124, 129, 145-146, 149, 167

groans, 153

guilt, 11-12, 58, 75, 89-90, 93-94, 97, 136

H

heaven, 15, 51, 58, 60, 64-66, 100, 141, 148, 164, 170, 172

hide, 57

hilasmos, 50, 53-54

holy, 4, 18, 29, 35, 58, 64, 87, 105, 124-125, 161

human, 13-14, 40, 91, 102, 110, 123-124, 130, 134

humility, 5, 25, 118, 159, 169

I

image, 46, 130-131, 135-136

intercede, 139-140, 145, 153-155, 157, 162

intermediary, 101, 139

interpretation, 3, 14, 46, 54, 56, 60, 145, 179

J

Jairus, 40

Job, 91

Joseph, 25, 105

judge, 36, 80, 130-131, 133-134, 148, 181

judgment, 75, 90, 96, 106, 142, 168, 172, 175-176

justification, 33, 85

K

kingdom, 75, 79, 117, 133, 166, 171, 173, 176

KJV, 49-50, 52-53, 110, 145, 152

L

lamb, 28, 56, 67, 84, 166

Law of Moses, 45, 62, 83

learn, 18

Louw and Nida, 53, 167

love, 82, 84, 142, 156, 180, 182

M

mediator, 146, 148

mercy, 35, 51-52, 54, 61, 67, 85, 87

Messiah, 26, 101, 117

metaphor, 39, 167, 179, 181

metaphysical, 20

Moses, 65, 74, 101, 105, 109, 126, 139, 148, 168

murder, 24, 158, 180

N

naked, 57, 60, 62

nature, 40, 110, 124-125

Nazareth, 114

Nicodemus, 30

NIV, ii, 3, 18, 51-53, 99, 145

Noah, 46

O

obedience, 121, 127, 181

Origen, 6

P

parakletos, 146, 153, 155

paralytic, 140

perfected, 123-124, 135

Peter, 156

Pharisee, 50

Philip, 128

pleading, 27, 41, 108, 139, 151, 154

price, 13, 42, 122, 167

priest, 46, 158, 161

propitiation, 49

punish, 8, 11-12, 75, 80, 169

R

ransom, 6-7, 147-148

reconciled, 139, 158

repentance, 135, 159

representative, 147, 160

resurrection, 33-34, 90, 96, 139, 156, 168

ritual, 46, 158

S

sacrifice, 26, 28, 38, 44, 48, 66, 158-159

salvation, 25, 96, 147, 167, 174

salvation process, 136

satisfaction, 8

saved by works, 90, 125

savior, 99, 133, 147, 181

scapegoat, 26

Sea of Galilee, 118

seed, 40

shadow, 64

sheep, 38, 80, 167

sin, 29, 83, 86, 89, 91, 94, 155, 157, 180

sinless, 29, 93, 100, 123, 134

sorrow, 107, 119

spirit, 113, 121, 151

Stephen, 24, 141

substitution, 8, 11, 19, 33

symbolic, 123
sympathize, 61, 100-101

T

tabernacle, 65, 164
tax collector, 50
temptation, 39, 111, 115, 117, 120, 134, 156-157, 175
testimony, 147
throne, 58, 65, 165, 173
transaction, 2, 18, 32, 35, 43, 70, 72
transform, 95-96
translators, 50-52, 55, 145-146, 152

U

unjust, 11

V

vinedresser, 108
vineyard, 104, 108
vision, 58

W

will, 40, 96, 119, 166
wolf, 39
word, 9, 38, 91, 101, 125-126, 129
worship, 69, 113, 127, 166
worthy, 165

Acknowledgements

This study was developed over a number of years. Early forms of it were presented at many different Bible schools, and then as a series of articles in a magazine in the USA called the Christadelphian Tidings. Over the years I have received valuable input and feedback from many people whose influence can be felt throughout. At the risk of embarrassing them, I will name Judi Davis, Dave Garnand, Tim Genders, Norm Fadelle, Kathleen Fisher, Paul Launchbury, Tony Moore, Anthony Oosthuizen, Simon Peyton Jones, John Pople, Ted Sleeper, Nancy Sharp, Don Styles, and Mark Vincent. The sketches were drawn by Zoë Launchbury.

I especially thank my family, Rachel, Zoë, and Nate, for their ideas and suggestions, and for putting up with this project that has absorbed so much time over so many years.

To all who have helped me I offer my heartfelt thanks. To the extent that this work is successful, it is due to the hand of God behind so many wonderful people. Any shortcomings or failures are my own.

About the author

Dr John Launchbury was educated in Oxford and Glasgow, UK. As a professor in computer science he has won awards for teaching, and his research is respected worldwide. Now he brings that same inquisitiveness and clarity of thought to a Biblical topic that is often shrouded in mystery and complication. John lives in Portland, Oregon with his wife and two children.

Made in the USA
Middletown, DE
01 September 2018